THE
FINANCIAL
PROFESSIONAL'S
GUIDE TO
COMMUNICATION

THE FINANCIAL PROFESSIONAL'S GUIDE TO COMMUNICATION

HOW TO STRENGTHEN CLIENT RELATIONSHIPS AND BUILD NEW ONES

Robert L. Finder, Jr.

Vice President, Publisher: Tim Moore
Associate Publisher and Director of Marketing: Amy Neidlinger
Executive Editor: Jim Boyd
Editorial Assistant: Pamela Boland
Development Editor: Russ Hall
Operations Specialist: Jodi Kemper
Marketing Manager: Megan Graue
Cover Designer: Chuti Prasertsith
Managing Editor: Kristy Hart
Project Editor: Betsy Harris
Copy Editor: Geneil Breeze
Proofreader: Debbie Williams
Senior Indexer: Cheryl Lenser
Senior Compositor: Gloria Schurick
Manufacturing Buyer: Dan Uhrig

© 2013 by Pearson Education, Inc.

Publishing as FT Press

Upper Saddle River, New Jersey 07458

FT Press offers excellent discounts on this book when ordered in quantity for bulk purchases or special sales. For more information, please contact U.S. Corporate and Government Sales, 1-800-382-3419, corpsales@pearsontechgroup.com. For sales outside the U.S., please contact International Sales at international@pearsoned.com.

Company and product names mentioned herein are the trademarks or registered trademarks of their respective owners.

First Printing October 2012

ISBN-10: 0-13-301790-7
ISBN-13: 978-0-13-301790-8

Pearson Education LTD.
Pearson Education Australia PTY, Limited.
Pearson Education Singapore, Pte. Ltd.
Pearson Education Asia, Ltd.
Pearson Education Canada, Ltd.
Pearson Educación de Mexico, S.A. de C.V.
Pearson Education—Japan
Pearson Education Malaysia, Pte. Ltd.

Library of Congress Cataloging-in-Publication Data

Finder, Robert L., 1955-

The financial professional's guide to communication : how to strengthen client relationships and build new ones / Robert L. Finder, Jr.

pages cm

Includes bibliographical references.

ISBN 978-0-13-301790-8 (hardback : alk. paper) — ISBN 0-13-301790-7   1. Financial planners. 2. Customer relations. 3. Business communication. I. Title.

HG179.5.F5666 2012

332.1068'8—dc23

2012030548

To all financial professionals helping their clients succeed financially.

Contents

Acknowledgments

I would like to thank David Kowach, Chip Walker, and Andy Byer for their encouragement and unwavering support of this project.

Executive Editor, Jim Boyd, at Pearson Education deserves my deepest thanks for not giving up on me, even though I was ready to. And thank you, Buff Dormeier, CMT, a colleague and much better author than me, for calling Jim and suggesting that he consider my idea for this book. I hope that Jim has forgiven you by now. Betsy Harris and all the other remarkable professionals at Pearson Education have my admiration and appreciation for their superb editorial assistance.

Without Michael Thomsett's guidance, direction, and mentorship, this book never would have happened. A new book is very nice; a new and very dear friend is priceless.

To Patrick Koelle, my long-time colleague, coach, and good friend, thank you for keeping me in line and always trying to make me better—I know you have your work cut out. And thank you, Lisa Koelle—who in her own right is a consummate financial professional—for sharing so much of Patrick with me.

But this book would not have been possible without my wife Ginger's love, understanding, and support.

About the Author

Robert L. Finder, Jr., is a Managing Director for a national financial services firm, working closely with financial professionals to develop wealth management solutions for high net worth individuals and their families, businesses, institutions, and retirement funds. He was previously Executive Director of Wealth Management Solutions at Prudential Investments in Newark, NJ, and also served as National Sales Manager for the Managed Accounts Consulting Group. Mr. Finder was President and Chief Executive Officer of Johnson Heritage Trust Company in Racine, WI, and Landmark Trust Company in St. Louis, MO. Prior to that, he practiced estate planning and tax law.

He earned the designations of Certified Investment Management Analyst (CIMA) and Certified Investment Strategist (CIS) from the Investment Management Consultants' Association. Mr. Finder holds a B.A. in international relations from Memphis State University and a J.D. and LL.M. in taxation from Washington University School of Law.

The Power of the Dance

Life is the dancer and you are the dance.
—Eckhart Tolle, *A New Earth: Awakening to Your Life's Purpose*, 2005

After absorbing the ideas in this book, you will never again communicate nor define yourself as you once did. Your clients see and listen to you as never before. Your counsel has never been clearer or more clearly understood. You are more attuned to your clients and your ability to serve them. You exude passion and conviction; your emotions are contagious, your professionalism unmatched. Go ahead, pinch yourself—it's true—you're finally learning to dance.

Throughout your career you've been following directions, taking one step then another, doing what you were taught, what you learned, and what you do the best. But something was missing until now—your *identity*. You befriended your clients, but never as best friends. You filled the part, but never played the role. You spoke of facts, but your words lacked feelings. You sought self-control, but faltered in self-absorption.

The movement of your body is now in rhythm with your speech. Your facial expressions receive and emit emotion. You express and share ideas with ease. You relish the interaction. Practice and performance have merged into one. You communicate with your clients at a highly evolved state.

You hear your clients as you would wish to be heard. You understand their fears and concerns; their dreams and hopes are yours. You're committed to learning about your clients without prying or intruding. You inquire simply, devoting your attention to their answers not the formulation of your questions. You prove that you listen and energy flows freely between you. Your clients confide in you. Their trust and respect for you grows, and your relationships strengthen and flourish. Critical listening is a fundamental element of your communications.

You connect with your clients no matter the venue size. You extend an arm toward your client as you cast your eyes upon them and hold the contact as you deliver and complete your point. You look and dress the part—successful, impressive, classy, and respectful. You're firmly grounded whether seated or standing, and you gesture with ease and in synchrony with your message. You see and are seen in a new light.

Your voice projects not merely words, but emotions. You vary your pace and your tone for full effect. You let yourself pause—to think, to reflect, and to recharge; you let yourself pause—to pique your clients' curiosity, to draw them closer, to let them absorb. And you respect your clients and yourself by expunging non-words and hedge words from your speech. You have found your voice.

You understand that while style is critical, so is command of substance. You've perfected clear and concise explanations of recurring subjects in plain, simple English, and enveloped them with the facts and feelings relating to each client's case to make them relevant. You support your position with statistics and analytics, patiently teaching instead of bewildering, and you paint visual imagery with your stories, analogies, and personal experiences that touch your clients' hearts and minds.

You are proud to explain what you bring to each client relationship. You trust your disciplined process to find wealth management solutions in each of the four cornerstones, and you are committed to helping your clients build, manage, protect, and transition their wealth.

Your mastery of the critical elements of communication bestows upon you great power to exert on behalf of your clients. You use that power wisely and always in your clients' best interests—with care, skill, and caution—to help them succeed financially.

Indeed, you *are* ready. You are now going to learn how to dance.

Chapter 1

Defining Your Core

A value proposition is really just meaningless jargon and babble that doesn't do a thing for me or my clients.
—Financial professional's common lament

Perhaps you agree with this quotation. And you're confused that a book about communication skills for financial professionals would begin on a tired, worn, and seemingly insignificant subject.

It's a grave mistake to think of your value proposition in that way. To care so little about this fundamental statement that defines what you do, how you do it, and what you bring to each client relationship is to sell yourself woefully short and to deprive your clients of the true understanding of who you are and how you can help them achieve their financial goals and objectives.

Your value proposition is central to all communications with your clients. It serves as a compass guiding all of your interactions. It is a constant reminder to your clients—their North Star—of the importance of their relationship with you, and it is a constant reminder to

5

you—your North Star—of the duties and responsibilities you undertake to provide sound counsel and stewardship of your clients' financial affairs.

But still you may not be convinced. You recall in the past how you willingly submitted or were coerced (or both) to develop your own value proposition or to embrace your firm's. You struggled to infuse something unique and memorable on your own, and you struggled with the seemingly canned verbiage of the firm's.

While you tried to carry and present your colors, few clients were moved or impressed by your efforts, and you abandoned the value proposition as a means of rallying clients around your cause and you around theirs. And you found solace in your decision by the shared perception of so many of your colleagues who also give it cursory, if any, respect.

I understand your skepticism and negativity on the subject, if not your outright dismissal of the need for a value proposition. It's not your fault, however. The subject has been presented to you in the wrong way. I am going to change your mind.[1]

I have to ask you an important question, and this also is the starting point for your universal/core value proposition: What do you do?

What Do You Do?

In the space provided below, please write one sentence—
only one sentence—that defines the essence of what
you do.

```
┌─────────────────────────────────────────────┐
│                                             │
│                                             │
│                                             │
│                                             │
│                                             │
└─────────────────────────────────────────────┘
```

It didn't take you any time at all, did it? It was a
reflex action. It's engrained in your memory. And most
importantly, you're satisfied and proud of what it says
because it captures exactly what you do for your clients.

It's simple.

It's repeatable.

It's understandable.

Or, would you like to take another shot at it?

Suppose every day when you go to your office and
swipe your identification badge or scan your finger- or
retina-print in the biometric door lock to gain entry to
the building, you're greeted by a voice through the
intercom asking you to state why you've come to work?
Your response must be a single sentence, and it must
convey the essence of what you are there to do. What is
your response?

```
┌─────────────────────────────────────────────┐
│                                             │
│                                             │
│                                             │
│                                             │
└─────────────────────────────────────────────┘
```

And by the way, your response should be the same as everyone in your firm, large or small, from the chief executive or managing partner to the newest entry-level associate or member of the support staff. You're all there for a common purpose. Please, reread your response. Do you think the indicator light will turn green and allow you to enter?

Let's make it easier. What do you tell your kids or your parents when they ask you what you do for a living?

Did you write the same response in each of the three boxes? You should have.

Why would the responses be any different? They shouldn't.

Now please, consider the one sentence that captures the essence of what all financial professionals do:

I help my clients build, manage, protect, and transition wealth.

Compare that to what you wrote and to what I've heard from so many financial professionals—responses such as: "I help my clients live the one life they have." "I take the mystery out of investments." "I ask people a lot of questions and explain how financial things work." "I help clients sleep at night." "I help people plan for a secure retirement." "I'm my clients' financial go-to guy." "I help my clients achieve their goals and dreams." "I watch out for my clients." "I'm a financial quarterback." [I hate that one.]

The number of these one-liners that financial professionals proffer is seemingly endless. And few financial professionals are excited about adopting a colleague's similar description even though they're not very satisfied with their own. But what disturbs me most about these statements is the injustice they do to the well-intentioned financial professionals who utter them. Financial professionals, like you, who stand for so much more.

The difficulty we have in defining our role in the most basic and fundamental way is that someone, somewhere told us we had to come up with our own unique definition of what we do. They were wrong. Downright wrong.

As financial professionals we share a common purpose and that cannot be better said than "We help clients build, manage, protect, and transition wealth."

Now you're thinking, "What would be achieved if thousands of financial professionals just like me adopted such a simple statement? We would all sound the same." Except for those who held onto their clever individuality, you know the "I'm your financial quarter-back-types." That's the point.

Consider: A prospective client asks you, "What do you do?"

Response I—"I'm a financial quarterback."

Response II—"I help a select group of individuals, families, businesses, and institutions to build, manage, protect, and transition wealth."

Is there anything to argue about here?

But is that it? Hardly. That is the essence of the core/universal value proposition that I ask you to consider. It's the first of four key elements. The second element is to define the term "wealth."

The Four Cornerstones of Wealth

In the space provided below list the four critical cornerstones or disciplines of wealth:

1.	2.
3.	4.

This one shouldn't be too hard, but I'm surprised at how few of your clients understand that you can assist them in all of these areas. Perhaps that's because they have long perceived you as being concerned about and providing service in only one of these cornerstones.

For many of you, your clients look to you for assistance in managing their investments. They think of you as their investment advisor, or their stock guy (or gal), or their "broker." [Heaven forbid, and please if you call yourself a broker, stop, and if others call you that, stop them, too.] But do they realize—and what have you said or done to make them realize—that comprehensive wealth management is more than just investments?

Comprehensive wealth management also includes banking, credit, lending, and liability management.

But that's just half of the critical wealth management cornerstones. Another is risk management, which can be addressed through insurance and other asset protection strategies.

And you help your clients leave their legacies by providing guidance and assistance related to trusts, estates, and fiduciary services.

The four critical cornerstones of wealth are

1. Investments	2. Banking, credit, lending, and liability management
3. Risk management	4. Trust, estate, and fiduciary services

I begin defining wealth by describing the investment of a client's assets, not because of its paramount importance, but rather to make the point that while clients may think wealth and investments are synonymous, wealth includes much more. If financial professionals—especially those whose primary activities are focused on investments—fail to help their clients understand this, they will naturally gravitate to other financial professionals and other firms to receive the advice, services, and products they need related to the other three components of wealth.

See the bull's eye next to Investments in the following box?

1. Investments ◎	2. Banking, credit, lending, and liability management
3. Risk management	4. Trust, estate, and fiduciary services

That's there to remind financial professionals who think they only need to focus on their clients' investments that by sheer want and need at some time (and it usually comes sooner rather than later) their clients will seek out other financial professionals and firms to satisfy their needs in the other areas of wealth. And once they do so and relationships are established and cemented away from you, those other financial professionals and their firms will be aiming directly at the bull's eye on your back—at your relationship with your client—which you have placed in grave jeopardy with your singular focus.

In fairness to financial professionals who concentrate on investments, that bull's eye shifts to any of the other cornerstones of wealth when financial professionals specializing in those disciplines neglect to provide guidance and counsel on the other cornerstones.

To recap:

The first element of the core/universal value proposition is "build, manage, protect, and transition wealth."

The second element is to define wealth as comprehensive wealth management encompassing more than just investments. Comprehensive wealth management encompasses all aspects of investing, but also banking, credit, lending, and liability management; risk management through insurance and other asset protection strategies; and trust, estate, and fiduciary services.

The Third Element

The first and second elements describe what you do.

The third element describes how you do it.

Outline below the major steps of your wealth management process:

How did you describe the first step of your process?

"I analyze my client's situation." "I ask a lot of questions." "I deconstruct my client's portfolio." "I conduct a thorough risk posture assessment." "I assess my client's financial and tax status, their time horizon, and their investment objectives." "I develop a financial action plan for my clients."

Compare these responses and yours to: "I listen to my clients."

Listening, which is explored in depth in the next chapter, is a critical communication skill for financial professionals to master. When you listen to your clients, you learn. When your clients speak you gain an understanding that's impossible to attain when you're speaking.

Consider how clients will feel when they learn about how your process starts:

> Statement I—"First, I'll ask you to provide detailed financial information and then I'll ask you a lot of questions about your financial affairs."
>
> Statement II—"My process starts by listening to you."

Clients have been conditioned their entire lives to be spoken to. To be pitched. Turn the table. Give your clients what they yearn for: Respect, evidenced by your sincere and earnest desire to listen to them and to learn from them. Stop being so data-driven. You'll get the data you need in due course. Make it clear instead that you're interested in their story, not just their statements, documents, and policies. The experience will be much deeper and richer for both of you. And then you can go on and analyze the data they'll willingly share with you to your heart's content.

Which takes us to the next step in the process: the "go-to-work" phase. It's often cited as the "analysis" phase, but only rarely do financial professionals offer clients more than a glimpse of all the effort and thought that goes into this stage of the process. Why don't you let your clients know that with the information they share with you, you roll up your sleeves and go to work? You study and analyze the information. You consider various ways to address the client's issues and objectives, and you test and model those solutions until you arrive at a solution or set of solutions designed specifically for the client.

Consider how clients will feel when they learn:

Statement I—"I'll deconstruct the information we receive and identify any gaps or deficiencies in your plan that should be addressed."

Statement II—"Then I will go to work. With the information you've shared with me, I'll study and analyze it; I'll develop, model, and test various ways to meet your objectives; always seeking solutions customized to your needs."

After that point it's time to explain the third step in your process—the recommendations, advice, and solutions you have developed for your client—in plain, simple English. No technical jargon. And when you and your client reach agreement, you will implement those solutions in an independent, objective, and unbiased manner, always considering the importance of controlling costs and expenses.

Presentation skills are examined in later chapters. For now, just remember this: Clients don't want to be talked down to, and they don't want to be baffled by financial verbosity. They want straight talk they can understand. Let them know that's what they'll get from you.

They also want something else—to know that you're on their side, that you're looking out for their best interests. Let them know that you're an independent thinker who they can rely on for objective and unbiased advice. And that your compensation will be fair and reasonable in exchange for the services and products that you provide and that you are always considering ways to control their costs and expenses.

Consider how clients will react when they are told:

Statement I—"We'll then implement the plan."

Statement II—"We will explain our findings and present our recommendations to you in plain, simple English, no technical jargon, and when we reach agreement and put our recommendations into effect, we will do so in an independent, objective, and unbiased manner, always mindful of controlling costs and expenses."

The final step in your process is monitoring, evaluating, and adjusting the solutions that have been set in motion. But a word of caution: Never refer to this fourth step, as so many financial professionals do, as "the most important step." All the steps of the process are important, and weakness in any of the links undermines them all.

On an ongoing basis, you will monitor and evaluate the progress of the client's wealth management plans and make adjustments as necessary. You'll also make adjustments, as appropriate, as market conditions change, as tax laws and regulations are amended, and, of course, as changes occur in the lives of your clients and their families.

Consider how clients will react to the final step of your process:

> Statement I—"We'll tweak your plans as conditions warrant."
>
> Statement II—"We will then monitor, evaluate, and adjust. We'll monitor and evaluate the plans that have been put in place to make sure they're meeting expectations, and, if they're not, we'll take appropriate action. And we'll make adjustments to your plans as material changes in the markets warrant, as changes occur in tax laws and regulations, and as changes inevitably occur in your life and the lives of your family."

To summarize your process—the third element of your value proposition:

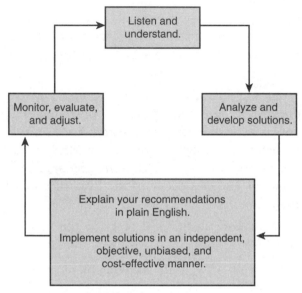

FIGURE 1.1   *Core wealth management process.*

The Fourth and Most Understated Element

Your client will now know what you do (elements 1 and 2) and how you do it (element 3). That gives rise to the fourth element—explaining why you're confident in your ability to do so.

Surprisingly, most financial professionals are very shy or too humble when it comes to explaining the fourth element—the "say something nice about your-self" element. Perhaps it's because they don't want to come across as braggadocios or arrogant, which I understand. But doesn't a client want to know that you have what it takes to serve his or her needs? Doesn't a client want to know of the pride you take in your edu-cation, advanced training, and commitment to ongoing professional development? Doesn't a client want to know that you bring not only your experience, but also your judgment to the relationship, which you exercise with care, skill, and caution? And doesn't the client want to know that you have the resources of your firm supporting you, and you have the resourcefulness to draw upon fellow experts, internally and externally, to help meet any of your clients' wealth management needs? Of course they do. And don't they want to know that you bring an unwavering passion, commitment, and dedication to your work, singularly and collec-tively, focused on helping your clients succeed finan-cially? Most certainly. Then tell them.

There was a TV series in the late 1970s titled *The Guns of Will Sonnett*, starring Walter Brennan as a crusty old gunslinger. Will Sonnett was never one to miss an opportunity to let others know that, while his son and grandson were very quick-draws and expert marksmen, he was better than both of them. "No brag, just fact," he would say.

It would be good, if all financial professionals had just a touch more Will Sonnett in them. Let your clients know what you bring to your relationships. If you don't, who will?

Consider a client's reaction upon being told:

Response I—"I strive to deliver exceptional service in a timely and professional manner to meet or exceed your expectations."

Response II—"I am proud of the education, advanced training, and ongoing commitment to professional development that I bring to each client relationship. In addition to my experience I also render my judgment with care, skill, and caution on behalf of my clients. I have the resources of my firm to support me, and I have the resourcefulness to draw upon fellow experts within or outside the firm whenever necessary to help meet the needs of my clients. And I do this with a passion, commitment, and dedication to helping my clients and their families succeed financially."

No brag, just fact.

The Fifth Element

Under special circumstances it may be appropriate to add a *fifth* element to your value proposition—an intensely personal element based on your own experiences in life and in your profession. The fifth element explains not what you do, how you do it, or why you're good at it. It says more—more about the type of person you are—your character, purpose, and principles. It gives a client a profound and deeper sense of what they should expect from a relationship with you. I'm going to hold off saying more about the fifth element for now, because it requires you first to master the skills of *critical listening*.

Endnote

1. Before proceeding, let me give you a brief explanation of style I use throughout this book. My comments are addressed directly to "you" or to the "financial professional," but this encompasses everyone on your team as well.

   The same qualifier relates to my references to the "client." This also encompasses your communication with a *prospective* client, more than one client, or a roomful of people. Here again, I keep my style on a one-to-one basis, but it all applies to a broad "client universe."

Chapter 2

The Secret of
Listening...*Critically*

*When someone is speaking to me, am I listening or am
I just waiting to speak?*

*You know, I have to admit, I'm usually just waiting to
speak, but I know I should be listening.*

—Financial professional's common lament II

Almost all financial professionals say that listening is a critical communication skill. They say that listening to their clients is essential to developing new relationships and solidifying and enhancing existing ones. And most financial professionals say that they are above average listeners just like in *Lake Wobegon* where "all the women are strong, all the men are good looking, and all the children are above average."

It's an interesting exercise to rate the listening aptitude of other individuals: your spouse or partner; your children; your friends and your best friends; colleagues and business associates; management of your firm; and of course, your clients and prospective clients. Who are the better listeners and what makes them so?

Turnabout is fair play, so how do you think these same people would rate your listening aptitude? Be honest. Why aren't you perceived as a better listener? And what if you were; would it matter? Yes, it would, and it would matter volumes.

When I ask financial professionals what their clients would say about them, an almost universal response is, "My clients know I care about them." Financial professionals may say that they care, but actions speak louder than words. Consider what you demonstrate and learn from listening combined with the simplest choice of words. The potential is a financial professional's bonanza.

When I ask financial professionals if they would rather be known as a great speaker or a great listener, the vast majority respond: great speaker. To be able to inspire and influence, to turn paralysis into action, to provide sound counsel and advice creates a rush, an ego boost, one of the ultimate highs, and isn't that what it's all about?

Speaking is active; listening is passive, isn't it? You're expected to "do," not do nothing. What good is all your training and experience, if you're not going to share it with others who will benefit from your direction? I assume your Bucket List doesn't include making it into "Who's Who of Listening," but should it?

Besides, words are mightier than the sword. The real issue is whose words are the mightiest? Yours or your clients?

Your bias that favors speaking at the expense of listening is not your fault. Unfortunately, most financial professionals aren't as accomplished in this critical communication skill as they should be. I ask you to think about why financial professionals aren't better listeners.

Listening is innate. No one had to teach you to listen; absent a physiological disorder, you hear. And while you were taught how to speak, how to read, how to write, and how to think, hearing just happens. It doesn't get better with additional training and practice like learning a language or playing an instrument—or does it? And even if you sought training to improve your listening skills, where would you get it? It's not part of the traditional curriculum in most schools, nor has it been a core element of most professional training programs within the financial services industry.

Who Listens and Who Speaks?

Listening is what buyers do, not sellers. It's part of our culture. Sellers present the value of their goods and services and buyers listen. They consider what the seller has presented, perhaps ask a few questions, and then listen some more to the seller's response. Armed with the information the seller provides, the buyer makes the decision to buy or to seek other options from other sellers. Overly simplistic, perhaps, but you've been on the buyer's side of the coin as much as or more than you've been on the seller's, so you know what it's like. Buyers— that is, *your clients*—have simply been conditioned to listen to you speak.

Listening takes time and patience. And time is your most precious and scarce commodity. With such high demands on your time, you have to make a choice. Either you speak or your client speaks. Sure you want to learn as much as you can about your client, not just to comply with regulatory and fiduciary standards of conduct, but because it's the right thing to do. But constrained as you are by the clock, when it boils down to getting your message across or listening to the client, you too often pay lip service to the latter. Besides you may not get another opportunity to say what you want to say, and no one ever engaged your services or bought your products because they talked themselves into doing so, or might they if given the chance?

Listening doesn't matter if you don't care. That's pretty strong, and I don't mean to suggest that you don't care about your clients; you may simply not care enough about them to be a good listener for a number of reasons. All clients say just about the same thing ("I want more return with less risk," or "We want to preserve principal, generate sufficient cash flow, and grow our assets."). Or, you've perfected your approach to selling and relationship building, and it's worked nicely over time, so why mess with success? Listening can get pretty "touchy-feely," and if it's not your style to delve without reservation or precondition into a client's situation, so be it.

And let's face it, listening is a lot harder than it seems. You have a lot going on. Markets to study and keep an eye on, proposals to generate, reviews to prepare, calls to return, e-mails to answer, problems to resolve, a constant stream of conference calls and meetings...it never stops, and that doesn't even begin to account for the demands on your time and energy from your family, church, community, and personal interests and hobbies. Fortunately when clients are speaking to you, they speak at a rate that your brain can easily process giving you ample excess capacity to multitask as you're listening to them. Not good.

If you're still not convinced that listening to your clients is critical, how often have your clients told you that you listen to them "too much"?

Remember the popular ad that E. F. Hutton & Co. used to run: "When E. F. Hutton speaks people listen." Catchy slogan—horrible message. Actually just before the firm was acquired by Shearson Lehman Brothers, they reversed the slogan to "E. F. Hutton—When our clients speak, we listen." Unfortunately, the slogan didn't survive under new management (but then again, neither did they).

And lest we never forget the Golden Rule: Do unto others as you would have them do unto you. Imagine that you're the client. How does it feel to be talked at or lectured to, unable to get a word in edge-wise? All you want is someone to help you if only they would stop and listen to your ideas and feelings, to take you seriously, and to demonstrate that what you tell them matters.

Think of all the expressions that should remind you of the importance of listening:

Now hear this	Listen up
Are you listening?	Pay attention
Hear ye, hear ye	Words fell on deaf ears
Inquiring minds want to know	
Let the man speak	Speak up
Hear the man out	Tin ear
Open your ears	You haven't heard a word
Listen between the lines	
You have two ears and one mouth: Use them in that proportion	

But what kind of listener are you?

Are you a "non-starter"? Do you pretend to be interested in what the client has to say, but you never quite seem to allow them to tell you because your lead-ins morph into self-promotional presentations?

Are you a "fact-finder"? Do you capture vast amounts of factual information and data, especially anything relating to the number and type of accounts, account values, and performance, but avoid topics that are more subjective or emotional?

Are you an "iceberg listener," on watch for the first signs of a problem you're able to address to the exclusion of other problems (or opportunities) that you leave unexposed?

Are you the "judge," agreeing or disagreeing with your clients, and if you disagree, setting them straight?

Are you a "pretender"? You try to listen to your clients, but you're just not that into them. Your approach is mechanical. It feels forced. You find yourself wandering at times. Thinking about ways to speed things along. Thinking about what to ask next. Thinking when will this end. Pretenders aren't very comfortable listeners, and their clients can tell (but they won't).

There may be some of each of these listening types in all financial professionals, but self-awareness helps you control these tendencies. It's far more effective to be a fully engaged, patient, and respectful listener. And that's what your clients want, too.

Improving Your Listening Skills

No one would argue the importance of being prepared: not the Boy Scouts, the New York Giants, the Red Cross, the Coast Guard, and certainly not financial professionals. Preparation is evidenced in many ways: mental and physical readiness to anticipate and deal with any accident or situation that may occur; repeated drills and simulations to sharpen skills and senses when faced with actual threats and volatile conditions; and game plans and response protocols to address reasonably anticipated contingencies. For many financial professionals the preparation of an agenda signals their desire to face head-on the topics and subjects that they believe are most relevant to the client for whose benefit the agenda was purportedly designed. An agenda is a sign of respect and professionalism, but it's also a sign, potentially, of grave danger. How can such a well-intended and thoughtful work-product as an agenda go awry? Easy.

By stubborn, steadfast adherence to an agenda, financial professionals can stifle the listening process because it's their agenda—the second most important agenda. Too often the most important agenda—the client's—gets little, if any, attention because you insist on exerting too much control. Some of us are just outright control freaks. But why should you go to all the effort to put an agenda together if you're not going to talk about it? That makes no sense unless the primary reason for the agenda is simply to demonstrate you're prepared. And what's wrong with that? Everyone acknowledges preparation is good and being unprepared is bad.

Consider beginning your meeting with a straightforward declaration of preparedness supported by your agenda and any collateral materials:

> I'm fully prepared to discuss my comprehensive approach to wealth management: how we help a select group of families like yours build, manage, protect, and transition wealth. I've also drawn up an agenda that outlines key elements of my practice, philosophy, and process.

"Wow," the client thinks silently. "This guy is really prepared, and he's just like all the other financial professionals I've dealt with—he's really prepared to talk about himself. It must be something about all financial professionals. They just love to hear the sound of their own voices and hardly give a lick about what I have to say." But just as the client prepares to hunker down for a long-winded diatribe, interspersed with the occasional question that will be met with a terse response, you change the dynamic.

Like a wrestler with his opponent in his grips—but not quite—you intentionally release your grip and set your opponent free knowing that there will be a better time—the appropriate moment—later in the meeting—to reassert control.

Financial professionals can learn from this paradox—that you have to relinquish control to your client to build trust and strengthen the relationship.

You explain, "The purpose of this meeting is for us to focus on those matters that are most important to you." Pausing here is a good idea, because the client won't believe what he's hearing and will need a few seconds to digest this. And then continue, "Please, tell me what's on your mind?" You do not say another word in the deafening few seconds of silence likely to follow.

Then something remarkable will happen. Clients will begin sensing you're different and will start to open up. Slowly at first, because they're still not sure this is genuine; however, with appropriate nurturing and encouragement from you, clients will become more comfortable, more open, and more informative—allowing you to discover what's most important to them.

I call this a *Critical Opener* and it consists of three distinct parts:

1. A declarative statement of your readiness and preparation to explain what you do for your client followed by a pause, before shifting the focus away from yourself to the client.

2. Explain that, as always, the primary objective of the meeting is to focus on those matters that are most important to the client. After all, isn't that the purpose of the meeting?

3. The client is politely and directly invited to share his or her thoughts and perspectives.

Why is this approach so useful?

Imagine that you were responsible for designing and executing a battle plan, and you had virtually no fresh intelligence to base your plan on. What would you do? Hopefully, nothing. You certainly wouldn't launch an all-out attack on...what, a target or targets yet to be clearly identified?

Yet too many financial professionals can't resist launching a salvo of information at their clients without fresh intelligence. The beauty of how you gain intelligence is that it's not a stealth or covert process, it's a professional, respectful, and reliable process because it comes directly from the source.

Still not convinced? If you were playing poker, wouldn't you like to see everyone else's hand? Some players think they gain an edge by paying close attention to the body language and idiosyncrasies of other players, the "tell." Similarly, some financial professionals believe they can learn a lot about their clients and prospects by focusing on their body language, and much has been studied and written on that subject. [The benefits from those techniques are minimal, however, and the potential costs too great because it diverts your attention away from activities that are much more critical, that is, critical listening and critical questioning.] But don't be concerned about "stealing signs" that may or may not tell you what you want to know. If you want to know, don't guess or speculate—just ask them. Never works in a game of poker; almost always works with your clients, and there is never any harm in trying (except of course at the casino).

This was never made clearer to me than on the day I met Coach Atlas.

The Coach Atlas Experience

I used to be a pretty good tennis player. I played college tennis and then competitive amateur tennis at the national level. My goal was to someday win a "gold ball," signifying a national championship. I worked hard at my game and once or twice came close, but perhaps my shaky nerves—the dreaded "choke"—and my even shakier left leg were just too much to overcome. If six knee surgeries all on the same leg weren't enough, I thought I would blow out my Achilles tendon for good measure—same left leg. Now anyone with common sense would just have packed it in, but the dream of the gold ball remained, and I still believed I could do it with the right help.

With the Achilles tendon repair, I was non-weight bearing for several months, but I had the idea that during this downtime I could strengthen my core and upper body so that when I returned to competition, I would be better prepared in those two areas. But I realized that in my condition, I needed help and just coincidentally a new health club had opened near our house in Montclair, New Jersey. I called and explained my situation and inquired about their personal trainers. I didn't want to work with just anyone; I wanted a trainer who was highly experienced in dealing with serious athletes with physical issues and objectives like mine. To my delight I was told that the club had just the man, "Coach Atlas," and an appointment was set for the next day.

My wife, Ginger, accompanied me to the appointment, and I distinctly remember putting two blank checks in my wallet. Why do I remember that? Because I wanted so badly to come away from the meeting with an action plan that would help me pursue my dream, and I knew that if I signed up, Ginger would want her own fitness plan, because she's also very competitive.

Anyway, I hobbled into the club on my crutches with Ginger by my side, and the girl at the front desk directed us to have a seat in Coach Atlas's office, letting us know he would be with us shortly. I propped my leg up on another chair, and we waited for about 10 minutes before Coach Atlas walked in. He said virtually nothing to either of us, went over to his desk, opened a file drawer, pulled out two sheets of paper, and handed them to us. It was his C.V., which I quickly glanced at and read that he was a graduate of a college that I had never heard of but also that he graduated *"Magna Com Laud."* [That's right, he spelled it wrong.]

Then it happened: the "pitch." Coach Atlas told us all about the club's brand new, state-of-the art cardio equipment including stairmasters, elliptical trainers, the best treadmills made, and then he told us about all the features of their strength machines and their European-designed free weights section. He told us about Vo2 testing, the digital video running analysis, flexibility exams, plyometric workouts, and something that really sounded good to me, "turbulence training." Then he gave us a calendar full of classes of various types running continually from night to day, and on the back side was a price list for Gold, Diamond, and Platinum memberships. We also learned that Diamond and Platinum members received complimentary child day and evening care (even though we don't have children), and we learned how each member of the staff was there to make our experience exceptional.

Well, Coach Atlas certainly made this an exceptional experience. I remember during the Coach's unrelenting information dump, muttering to Ginger, but loud enough so Coach could hear it, "Does this guy give a damn about why we're here?" Oblivious to my remarks and the increasingly pained looks of disbelief and growing dislike for this individual, Coach Atlas persisted fully intending, I have no doubt, to cover every single point on his agenda until I finally interrupted him.

"Coach, Coach Atlas," I said, "there's not going to be any plyometrics or turbulence training. I don't need and I can't use your stairmasters and glockenspiels or whatever you called those things. Can't you see? Don't you understand I'm non-weight-bearing for three months? Do you care why we're even here?"

With that Coach Atlas went silent. I thought, the poor guy just got a little too exuberant about all the resources and capabilities he and the club had to offer, and he got ahead of himself. Surely, he sees the importance of changing the direction of this meeting. And surely he did.

He turned back to his desk, opened another drawer, took two sheets of paper out, handed them to Ginger and me, and said, "Perhaps you'd be more interested in our nutrition programs."

Honest to goodness, that's what he said. I couldn't make this stuff up.

And with that we politely took his handout, folded it up, and I told him, "Coach, thank you for your time. You've given us a lot to think about. We'll consider all of it and get back to you." Then I hobbled back out of the club on my crutches with Ginger at my side in total disbelief and amazement at what just happened.

I'll never forget Coach Atlas as I'm sure you'll never forget all the Coach Atlases you've experienced on the buy-side of your life. But imagine all that Coach Atlas had to say that day.

"Bob and Ginger, I'm fully prepared to tell you about the club, our equipment and facilities, and about my experience and approach to helping my clients achieve their personal fitness goals in a proven, safe, and effective manner. But, Bob, please tell me about your foot. What happened? I want to make sure I understand your situation and what you would like to

achieve. By sharing that with me, I promise, we'll focus on those matters that are most important to you. And then, Ginger, I want to know about you and what you would like to work on so that we can also discuss what's important to you."

How do you think I would have felt (or how Ginger would have felt) had Coach Atlas used this critical opener with us? I'll tell you, he could have read it verbatim right out of a book like this, and I wouldn't have cared. And, Coach, if you're out there please let me know and I'll send you a copy, no charge, because you need it dearly. I had a story to tell. My story. It was all about me, just like it needs to be all about your clients. And Ginger had her own story to tell. I know she would have told him, "Look, I don't care what this is going to cost. You can't imagine how much money he's spent on his tennis over the years. What I want to make sure is that he rehabs properly and doesn't do anything else to compound his physical problems. If you can help him I'm all for it, but just make sure it's a very sound and supervised approach. And as for me personally...."

And guess what? I wouldn't have cared about the cost of whatever fitness program Ginger ultimately chose. It wasn't about money. It was about finding someone who cared, someone who listened.

This was a personal experience from a would-be client's perspective. What follows is my personal experience but from the financial professional's perspective.

We had made it to the finals for a competitive, high stakes and high profile client—an institution with an endowment of more than $100 million. We were given

20 minutes for our presentation, which may seem unreasonable because there was so much to cover, but I relished the opportunity and the challenge as I believe that 20 minutes is just about the maximum attention span of an individual.

We had a lot going for us: a very good relationship with the chairman of the investment committee who had shared vast amounts of information about the organization, its accomplishments, and its vision for the future. We had learned about the makeup of the investment committee and the management of the organization. We were well-versed on their current financial situation, and we were proposing a creative suite of services and products to address their needs in a cost-effective manner. All the stars had aligned in our favor, so it seemed, until the day of the presentation when we received a call informing us that the chairman had to attend to a serious family issue and would not be attending the meeting, but that the meeting would take place as scheduled.

No problem. We were ready. We were prepared and we had practiced. It was "showtime."

We didn't even think about using a Critical Opener to begin the presentation because of the time constraints. Besides, we knew everything we needed to know, and we were sure all the firms bidding for this relationship were fully capable for the assignment. Why else would we all be in the "finals"? Therefore, our approach was to distinguish ourselves by making the most impactful and memorable presentation possible.

While we hadn't planned for the chairman not to be at the meeting, our problem turned out to be the individual who ran the meeting in his place, Alexander Lyon. Looking back, the Chairman had mentioned Mr. Lyon to us during one of our previous discussions. He told us he had a very strong personality and a strong sense of what to do in just about every situation. But our pre-presentation research, while extensive, did not include any specific inquiries about Mr. Lyon.

The presentation began. Oh, how I loved that presentation, perhaps the most innovative I had ever developed for a case like this. Then it happened. I said it. I didn't mean to say it, it just slipped out. I thought no one heard it or cared. And I assured myself it wouldn't slip out again: my reference to the "efficient frontier."

Too late, Mr. Lyon heard it and Mr. Lyon roared!

"All you financial consultants are alike. Just a bunch of CYA statisticians afraid to speak your mind and take a position. You flood us with graphs and charts and studies and research, and at the end of the day you haven't done squat. Let me tell you what I've done for this endowment...."

While my repeated efforts to explain and redeem myself were drowned out by Lyon's roar, I could at least be thankful that this pain would only be endured for another 15 minutes.

Thirty minutes later, despite repeated attempts to reclaim just a modicum of respect, Lyon was still roaring.

That was it; I had had enough. Now I just wanted to fight back. I wanted to tell Lyon off. We obviously weren't going to win this one, so why not at least feel better? But professionalism and decorum prevailed, and finally, mercifully the meeting ended.

As we exited the building into the bright afternoon sunshine, I asked my colleagues if there was a nearby establishment where we might find "refreshment" in hopes of refortifying our badly bruised and beaten egos. I needed a drink.

That's when my colleague looked at me and said, "How'd you think it went?"

"How do you think it went! Are you kidding [and he wasn't]? That was the worst experience I've had in my entire professional career. Are you serious?"

That's when our other colleague chimed in, "I thought it went pretty well."

A few minutes later as I waited for my double Campari and soda, I asked myself "How did I let that happen? What could I have done differently?" And the answer then was obvious. Too late, but obvious: a Critical Opener.

"Ladies and Gentlemen, my partners and I are fully prepared to explain how our comprehensive approach to wealth management can serve you and the endowment in a prudent and cost-effective manner; however, to be certain that we make the best use of your time this afternoon, please share with us your thoughts and perspective on the stewardship of the Organization's assets. By doing so, we promise that we'll focus on the matters that are most important to you, Mr. Lyon."

Now Lyon would still have roared, I have no doubt of that, but at least we would have known where he was coming from, and we would have had the option of adjusting our presentation accordingly. Instead, we walked right into Lyon's den like three big, fat, juicy zebras.

In Lieu of the Standard Opener

While I thought my presentation described in the fiasco above was great, it paled in comparison to the labor of love that another colleague of mine put into a presentation that he asked me to help him deliver to an investment board half a continent away from Lyon country. He had been courting this relationship for more than two years, and finally his opportunity came to present in another finals against formidable competition. His presentation materials were extensive. He prepared a multi-tabbed binder elaborating on major points that he also eloquently addressed in his response to the RFP. When we met to discuss the presentation format, he told me that he would like to begin by addressing tabs 1 and 2 and then he would ask me to cover tabs 3 through 5. He would wrap up with tabs 6 through 9 and hopefully there would be some time left for questions.

He was so proud of his work and so eager to give the presentation, it was hard to tell him he needed to begin with a Critical Opener, but I did. I think he was actually hurt by it. He put so much work into the presentation, and now I was telling him that we should be prepared to go off script. He didn't understand. But with a bit of arm-twisting he relented, and we practiced his delivery of a Critical Opener until he was comfortable with it. He delivered it as we rehearsed, but he also gave it "his own voice."

Then an amazing thing happened. Each of the board members opened up and shared their thoughts and ideas.

"I'm having trouble understanding why we're paying so much for these money managers when all we seem to do is fire two or three of them each year and replace them with the next 'best money manager,' only to find ourselves in the same position a few years down the road firing them. Seems we're not getting what we want from our money managers, so why don't we just index the darn portfolio and save ourselves a bunch of trouble—and some money too?"

Another board member expressed concern about the stability of the firm that would provide the services they were seeking as well as the stability of the team of financial professionals who would be delivering those services.

"I want to understand your capability to provide socially responsible investment management services," added another board member, and we received several other comments relating to our investment outlook and the role of alternative investments in the portfolio.

Any surprises? Not really.

Good to know what was on the board's mind? Are you kidding?

We were fully prepared to address all of their points and more, except the order in which they were presented in my colleague's materials would have been quite different, and we might have—would have—touched on a bunch of related or ancillary matters—of great importance, I'm sure—along the way. And no doubt we would have sounded just like our competitors who also came in well-prepared and were intent on proving it, no matter what the prospective client wanted to hear.

The board showed us their hands. And why wouldn't they? This wasn't a game of poker. We sat on the same side of the table [I hate that cliché] with them. The Critical Opener revealed what was most important to them and more. It revealed that we cared, that we listen to our clients, and that we address their needs, not what we perceive their needs to be.

My colleague won that relationship and many other financial professionals like him who use Critical Openings with their clients have built and strengthened client relationships with this simple technique.

A final word on the Critical Opener: Find your own words, "your own voice." Of course, my words will seem "canned" to you. However, once you master the three elements of the Critical Opener you'll naturally find you own voice, and if you're down around Amarillo it might sound something like this:

"Son, I'm here to kick-start this donkey for you, but you might have some other fish to fry. So if you'd start us off, we'll get right to it and scratch that itch first. Then, I'll show you a deal that's so bodacious, you'll want to slap your mama."

Well, you get the idea.

Chapter 3

"Your Financial Professional Will See and Hear You Differently Now"

Doctors can be frustrating. You wait a month-and-a-half for an appointment, and he says, "I wish you'd come to me sooner."
—Comedy routine

Before addressing what comes after your Critical Opening, answer this question: How do people perceive you?

Are you more apt to be associated with these words:

Broker   Salesman   Business   Customers

Or these:

Advisor   Consultant   Practice   Clients

The latter series is typically associated with professionals such as doctors, attorneys, and accountants although financial professionals would also apply. Unfortunately, we often are referred to in terms of the former, especially for those of us who specialize in the investment element of comprehensive wealth management.

By connotation the words broker, salesman, business, and customers place undue pressure on financial professionals to sell. But words like advisor, consultant, practice, and clients—words that could easily define a physician—don't conjure up thoughts of selling or salesmanship, but rather of core clinical skills.

Core clinical skills are essential to any vibrant and growing practice—medical, legal, or financial. And the most fundamental of all clinical skills is the ability to interview and communicate with clients. Think about the number of interactions that you have with clients during the course of a year. Now multiply that over the course of a 30- or 40-year career. The number is staggering, yet for many financial professionals (and doctors and lawyers and others) core clinical skills often take a back seat to more objective activities of the profession such as diagnosing and solving problems.

A study in the *Journal of the American Board of Family Medicine* noted that "when patients are informed and involved in decision-making, they are more adherent to medical recommendations, and carry out more health-related behavior changes (e.g., exercise, smoking cessation and dietary modifications)."[1] The study concluded that communicative or "therapeutic" relationships engendered greater trust in a patient's doctor. And as a result the study inferred that on a short-term basis patients will have greater recall of their discussions with their doctor, be more satisfied with the relationship with their doctor, and have a stronger inclination to comply with the recommended course of treatment. On an intermediate-term basis, patient compliance with the recommended treatment regimen should continue, and longer-term, the patients' symptoms, health, and quality of life may all improve.

Physician behaviors that build greater trust include

- Empathy and expression of intellectual appreciation of a patient's situation

- Statements of reassurance, support, and encouragement of patient questions

- Allowing the patient's point of view to guide the conversation in the concluding part of the office visit

- Expression of positive reinforcement or good feelings in regard to patient actions, possessions, or self

- Addressing social relations, feelings, and emotions of the patient and asking questions about such matters

- Increased time on health education

- Discussion of treatment effects

- Receptivity to patient questions and statements

- Summarization, talking at the patient's level, and clarifying statements

- Increased encounter time and more time spent on history taking

The following behaviors impair trust in the doctor-patient relationship:

- High rates of biomedical questioning
- One-way information flow (information collection without feedback)
- Utterances concerning the patient's experience or dismissing of those experiences
- Directive and antagonistic behavior
- Interruptions
- Dominance

Consider these two lists of behavior again—I've replaced the medical references and inserted references applicable to financial professionals—and ask yourself which behaviors you evidence in your interactions with clients.

Positive behaviors such as the following:

- Empathy and expression of intellectual appreciation of a client's situation
- Statements of reassurance, support, and encouragement of client questions
- Allowing the client's point of view to guide the conversation in the concluding part of the meeting
- Expression of positive reinforcement or good feelings in regard to the client's actions, possessions, or self

- Addressing social relations, feelings, and emotions of the client and asking questions about such matters

- Increased time on financial education

- Discussion of effects of suggested plans of action

- Receptivity to client questions and statements

- Summarization, talking at the client's level and clarifying statements

- Increased encounter time and more time spent on history taking

Negative behaviors such as the following:

- High rates of financial questioning

- One-way information flow (information collection without feedback)

- Utterances concerning the client's experience or dismissing of those experiences

- Directive and antagonistic behavior

- Interruptions

- Dominance

While the study asserted that behavioral change is a possible and realistic goal for physicians, it also noted the difficulty of the task given the encroachment of technology on communication skills and the complexity of medicine.[2] A more current exposé on the topic endorsed the need for more "therapeutic relationships" noting that "when patients reported that their doctors focused on their feelings and worries and listened to them carefully, they not only felt better but objective measures showed they had fewer symptoms of disease."[3] Again, substituting references to the medical profession for the financial profession, don't you agree with the following?

Clients need a financial professional who listens and who offers an explanation for what's happening that makes sense to them. Truly caring about the client is crucially important. The financial professional should help the client feel more in control of what's going on. When these ingredients are missing in financial encounters, clients may undermine their own financial health. Financial professionals often complain about "noncompliant" clients who fail to make recommended changes in their portfolio or bad habits like overspending or undersaving, but the problem may lie with the financial professional-client relationship.

One final point on this matter. I recently went to see my physician after I had a fainting spell on a flight home. It had been a very long day in which I squeezed in an hour-long workout in the hotel gym and dashed to the airport only to find my flight delayed for an hour. That fortuitously gave me time to grab a bite to eat since I had hardly eaten anything that day. Now if you only take one thing away from reading this book—and it's said that finding just a single idea that works may pay handsome dividends—then here's that one point of indispensable importance: Never ever order the double crab cakes and a cheap glass of Merlot at a restaurant/bar in the Cleveland Hopkins International

Airport and then board an RJ-145 and sit in the last row of the plane (window seat with obscured view) on a day with severe turbulence. And if that's too much to remember: Just don't order crab cakes and cheap wine in Cleveland.

Fortunately, all the tests he ordered—Echocardiogram and Holter monitor—turned out negative, and as suspected my culinary indiscretions no doubt led to my "spell" and related experience, which would be just too much information (my sincerest apologies to the gentleman in 15C).

But I wanted to ask the doctor if he thought some of my problem could also be stress-induced? Still typing into his laptop with passionate infatuation, he mumbled, "Perhaps," and kept right on typing. I could have dropped it at that and a minute later been back on my way to my stressful life, albeit with a clean bill of health. I wanted to prove a point, however, so I told him that I was writing this book, and it was stressful balancing that with my job and my home life, the latter of which I was neglecting badly. And then I told him that he's in the book. His typing stopped.

"I'm in the book? What's your book about?" he asked.

I told him it's about the importance of communications for financial professionals, but that it applies in many ways to all types of professionals including doctors. I explained that the art of personal communication is being trampled on by state of the art technology. "Take you and this office visit for example; you told me that your day has been very busy, one of your partners is on leave and another senior member of the group just announced his plans to retire. You're covering their caseloads, and it's just been crazy [although there was only one other person in the waiting room when I arrived—and when I left]. I asked about your sons, Mark and Brian, and if they've chosen a college yet, I believe I remember you telling me it was down to Virginia or Emory."

His facial expression and body language began to change, he even looked more human, less robotic.

I went on and told him about the power of critical listening. And guess what?

He asked me to tell him more about my book.

Endnotes

1. Rainer S. Beck, MD, Rebecca Daughtridge, and Philip D. Sloane, MD, MPH, "Physician-Patient Communication in the Primary Care Office," *Journal of the American Board of Family Practice* (January-February 2002), p. 25.

2. Rainer S. Beck, MD, Rebecca Daughtridge, and Philip D. Sloane, MD, MPH, "Physician-Patient Communication in the Primary Care Office," *Journal of the American Board of Family Practice* (January-February 2002), p. 36.

3. Shannon Brownlee, "The Doctor Will See You— If You're Quick," *Newsweek* (April 23-30, 2012), p. 48.

Chapter 4

Please, Tell Me More

Basically, I have been compelled by curiosity.
—Mary Leakey

I was pleased to tell my doctor more about my book, just as I would have been delighted to tell Coach Atlas about my tennis dreams, just as your clients are so willing to share their stories with you. In fact, if you're a good listener, you may be the only person they can talk to and confide in. All you have to do is ask and then encourage them to "Please tell me more."

Those four simple words will do more to reveal important and relevant information about your clients than anything else you can do or say. You can repeat it a dozen times and you know what will happen?

Sure, you say, "The client will stop and ask me if something's wrong—thinking maybe I'm stupid or something. Why do you keep repeating that silly phrase?"

Wrong. That will never happen. If you're sincere, your clients never even think about it because they will be so appreciative of the interest you're demonstrating, the respect you're giving them, and the self-restraint you're exercising unlike all the other financial professionals they've encountered throughout their lives. They'll simply keep telling you more.

Try it. Try it on your spouse, partner, or your kids. Try it on your colleagues and associates, friends and casual acquaintances. Try it on your doctor. And then, try it on your clients.

Is that it? Is that all there is to becoming a great listener?

A Critical Opener and this *simple request* are a good start, but you have to master two challenges: Exercise restraint and prove that you're listening

Don't interrupt. No matter how much you want to, don't. Never, not even to establish common ground with your client. "Oh, I know how you feel. That happened to me and let me tell you," or, "I have a lot of clients who have gone through the same thing." See how easy it is to step right back into the light at the expense of your client? Establishing common ground and common experiences are, of course, useful in building strong client relationships, but they can be more effective later. If you don't exercise restraint, there may not be a later.

Don't lose your focus. Don't start rehearsing what you're going to say when your client finishes. I know you can walk and chew gum at the same time and do an entire juggling routine at the same time, but listening and thinking about what you're going to say next doesn't work. You're going to miss something, perhaps a lot of important somethings. And turn off those distractions—your cell phone and CNBC—hold your calls and stop thinking ahead to your next meeting or plans for later in the day. Stay focused on the present. Stay focused on your client.

Don't start checking your mental rolodex of questions. Again, it requires you to work too hard and you have too much to lose in terms of information that your clients want you to understand. There will be time to ask questions. Now isn't that time. Try "Please tell me more" instead.

Don't interject your opinions and don't disagree or challenge your clients' thinking. You may be vehemently opposed to their position or reasoning. You may have proof positive that their information is mistaken or erroneous. You may have strong convictions that you feel obligated to express. Now is not the time. This time is about the client.

Don't filter what you hear. Financial professionals often have the mindset of Sergeant Joe Friday, from *Dragnet*, focused on "just the facts ma'am." You have to take it all in like a factual and emotional sponge. You'll have the opportunity later to wring out the relevant information, but until then, soak it all up—facts, feelings, emotions, ideas. Because good cops and good financial professionals take nothing for granted.

Don't panic if your client doesn't have a lot to say. Silence is golden, but not in this case. However, before peppering the client with a lot of questions in hopes that one will result in a breakthrough, or even worse, reverting to the comfort of your standard "pitch," try gently nudging your reticent client: "Tell me why this particular subject is so difficult for you to talk about." The client will recognize that you care and will be more apt to open up.

And don't go into "solution mode" as soon as your client has revealed an issue that you're more than able to address. You don't have to pick the lowest hanging fruit as shown in Figure 4.1. You've neither done your job, nor served your client well if you're satisfied with a token victory, and your client must have the multitude of their financial needs met by other financial professionals and firms. Exercise patience and in time you'll cultivate and harvest a bushel of wealth management opportunities (see Figure 4.2).

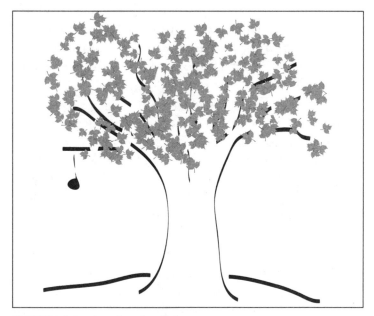

FIGURE 4.1   *Low-hanging fruit.*

FIGURE 4.2   *The abundant harvest.*

You're halfway home to becoming a great listener if you can exercise the requisite restraint, but to overcome the next critical listening challenge, it helps to be from Missouri.

> *I'm from Missouri—you'll have to show me.*
> —Phyllis Rossiter, Rural Missouri (1989)

You don't actually have to hail from Missouri to be a great listener, but it does help to keep in mind the unofficial state motto because listening requires proof. You need to prove to your clients and prospects that you are listening. Bobble-head doll-like financial professionals uttering the occasional, "Wow," "ah ha," or "Fantastic," don't get the job done. Think about the countless occasions when you were speaking to someone, at home, at the office, anywhere, and those are the responses you received. How did it make you feel? Like the other person couldn't care less about what you had to say, or worse, they couldn't care less about you.

Proving that you're a great listener takes concentration and energy.

If you're old like me, you may occasionally tune in to an "Easy Listening" music station. But there is no such thing as "easy listening" when it comes to building and strengthening client or any other type of personal relationship. You can't just switch it on or off. You have to be tuned to your client's station—their station in life, how they got there and where they see themselves and their family in years to come.

And while it's our patriotic duty to conserve energy and it's good for our financial self-interests, listening is energy intensive. But the good thing about consuming energy when you listen to your clients is that it costs very little and the returns are enormous.

So what is this skill that requires so much of your concentration and energy? You know it, you use it occasionally, but you've never developed its full potential: *feedback*. Affirmative proof that you hear what your clients are telling you. Feedback is evidence that you absorbed and digested what they said, verbal receipt acknowledging that what your client told you registered.

There are number of ways to provide feedback.

Reiterate
Echo
Repeat
Paraphrase
Playback
Summarize

You may not be ready to admit that you're not a master of these skills. So let me show you:

You have just delivered a heartfelt Critical Opener to a prospective client whom you're meeting with in your office. Now ask someone—anyone, it doesn't matter who—to read the following excerpt from their response. Tell them to read it at conversational speed and when they come to the direction to "PAUSE," ask them to stop. Then it's your turn. Prove you were listening to them and for good measure finish your response with a *simple request*—"Please tell me more."

Turn on the recording feature of your smartphone or any other recording device so you'll be able to assess your "performance" afterwards.

Stop!!! I didn't tell you to read the excerpt first. Your clients typically don't send you their prepared remarks like aides distribute to the Press Corps before a Presidential speaking engagement.

Okay, do you have your "client"? Give him or her the book and let them read the passage that follows once or twice to become more comfortable with it.

Everyone ready now? Then ask your client to read aloud:

> They are the principles on which my wife and I have tried to bring up our family. They are the principles in which my father believed and by which he governed his life. They are the principles, many of them, which I learned at my mother's knee. They point the way to usefulness and happiness in life, to courage and peace in death. If they mean to you what they mean to me, they may perhaps be helpful also to our sons for their guidance and inspiration.

> [Pause and let the listener provide feedback.]

> I believe in the supreme worth of the individual and in his right to life, liberty and the pursuit of happiness. I believe that every right implies a responsibility; every opportunity an obligation; every possession, a duty. I believe that the law was made for man and not man for the law; that government is the servant of the people and not their master. I believe in the dignity of labor, whether of head or hand; that the world owes no man a living but that it owes every man an opportunity to make a living. I believe that thrift is essential to well ordered living and that economy is a prime requisite of a sound financial structure, whether in government, business, or personal affairs.

[Pause and let the listener provide feedback.]

I believe that truth and justice are fundamental to an enduring social order. I believe in the sacredness of a promise, that a man's word should be as good as his bond, that character—not wealth or power or position—is of supreme worth.

[Pause and let the listener provide feedback.]

I believe in an all-wise and all-loving God, named by whatever name, and that the individual's highest fulfillment, greatest happiness, and widest usefulness are to be found in living in harmony with His will. I believe that love is the greatest thing in the world; that it alone can overcome hate; that right can and will triumph over might.

[Pause and let the listener provide feedback.]

These are the principles, however formulated for which all good men and women throughout the world, irrespective of race or creed, education, social position, or occupation, are standing, and for which many of them are suffering and dying. These are the principles upon which alone a new world recognizing the brotherhood of man and the fatherhood of God can be established.[1]

[Pause and let the listener provide feedback.]

Thank you, "client." Now let's debrief.

You're no doubt thinking, "Who was this person? My clients don't talk like that." Or, do you not give them the chance?

You might be wondering, "So what did this accomplish? I didn't find out how much money he has, how it's invested, who's advising him, or if he's pleased with their advice. Do I really care about this touchy-feely stuff? You'd think I had a Rockefeller in my office."

Well, in a way, you did—John D. Rockefeller, Jr., to be exact. And how do you think Mr. Rockefeller would have responded if you asserted your control, probed, and inquired into his financial affairs and told him how you and your team were ready, willing, and able to address any of his financial matters and concerns?

But by letting him speak and encouraging him to tell you more, you learned what matters most, and you began to create a bond, a connection, a trust between you that no questionnaire or line of questioning could ever establish.

However, what I'd like to know is would Rockefeller or the real "fellers" that you meet with on a regular basis have told you more? This Rockefeller was obligated to do so; your real clients and prospects aren't. Whether they will or not bears directly on the quality of your feedback.

So let's evaluate your feedback. Was it unresponsive, superficial, workmanlike, or attuned?

Unresponsive feedback is devoid of any material recall and acknowledgment of anything your client says. It consists of content-free, meaningless, and frequently repeated utterances such as "Ah ha," "I see," "Sure," "Wow," "Really," "Terrific," "That's great," and "Fantastic."

Superficial feedback attempts to acknowledge what the client says, without specific reference to what was said, and it's delivered in a manner that lacks sincerity and empathy: "That's interesting. Can you tell me a little more?"

Or consider the effect of "I know what you mean." It's not about knowing what your clients mean; it's about letting them know that you remember what they said.

Workmanlike feedback is a sign of competent listening with specific references to stated facts, feelings, and opinions that your clients have shared with you. But workmanlike feedback lacks the creativity associated with accurately paraphrasing what you heard. When you paraphrase, you explain what you heard, not just with the client's own words, but in your words that capture the essence of what the client conveyed, only perhaps in a more organized and logical manner. For example: "I understand that your parents taught you a lot" captures what Rockefeller said, but not the feelings and emotions revealed by the way he said it.

Attuned feedback is complete, deep, and responsive to what your clients say and how they feel. It is selfless feedback, completely client-centric, with no place for personal interjections and comments. It's empathetic listening of the highest order. It's not judging or evaluating or trying to interpret what is or isn't important—there will be another time for that and now is not that time—it's about unconditional attunement.

Imagine what you would want for yourself, or more importantly for someone dear to you when they had the opportunity to express themselves to someone who could make a meaningful difference in their lives. You would want for them attuned feedback, the same that your clients want and deserve from you.

Positive, genuine attuned feedback fosters discovery and exploration and builds trust, while negative or half-hearted feedback impairs the quality of client relationships, or worse still, keeps them from developing.

How was your feedback? Not as attuned as it could be? Why don't you try the exercise again, or better yet, try doing it differently, without someone playing the client. Go back and read Rockefeller's remarks to yourself a paragraph at a time. Feel free to read them several times if you wish. Then give yourself a few seconds and deliver your feedback.

Did the quality of your feedback improve? Hopefully it did, but consider this: When you read the remarks you did so at your own pace, and if you didn't understand something you could go back and reread it as many times as you wanted to improve your comprehension. You're not afforded that luxury when your real clients are speaking to you in real time. Listening is hard, and it requires you to focus and concentrate on what your clients are telling you. Where else should your focus and concentration be?

To summarize:

Use a Critical Opener to begin meetings with prospects and clients to let them know that you're fully prepared to discuss a particular subject. Send a clear and confident message letting your clients know you're ready to get down to business.

Then pause and remind your clients it's important that your time together be spent focusing on those matters—their agenda—that are most important to them and even more important than anything you've prepared for the meeting or planned to discuss.

And then politely and sincerely ask them to tell you what's on their mind.

Don't overthink your Critical Opener. Don't try to memorize it because you'll want to vary it slightly to fit each occasion. However, stick to a three-part framework that is simple, repeatable, and easy for your clients to understand.

1. **I'm prepared** to discuss whatever topics you deem pertinent;

2. But nothing is more pertinent than your client's agenda. That's the purpose of this meeting: **to focus on those matters that are most important to you;**

3. Let's begin, **Please tell me more about...**

Simple requests like "Please tell me what's on your mind," or "Please tell me about your current situation," may sound too generic, but think of them instead as "panoramic," opening a vista of information, feelings, problems, issues, and opportunities for you and your clients to explore.

Use *simple requests* liberally to encourage your clients to expand their remarks. "Please tell me more" is the universal wrench of effective communication, but you can also use "What else should I know," "Please go on," "Then what happened" to complement the always reliable and effective "Please tell me more."

Provide attuned feedback capturing not only the client's words but the client's feelings and emotions as well. And eliminate the all too common, awkward, repetitive, and annoying prefaces to your feedback such as: "So if I heard you correctly," "Let me see if I got this right," "What I think you're saying."

Take your time because your clients won't be upset with your few seconds of thought and reflection before receiving your feedback. They'll find it refreshing. Pausing to think is perfectly fine when you're actively listening or speaking. What's the rush? There isn't any, but when you're ready to offer your attuned feedback, **leave no doubt that you listened with your mind, your eyes, and your heart.**

Then remember to use another *simple request*, like "Please continue."

Couple your attuned feedback with a *simple request* to prove you listened to what your client has told you and to express your interest in learning more. **Or try reversing the order. Use a *simple request* to expand on your attuned feedback:** "Please tell me more about your parents. Their beliefs and values clearly left an indelible imprint on your life."

Then to let your clients know beyond a doubt how much what they have to say matters to you, **feed it all back to them,** just like I've done with this summary. They'll realize that you're different from all the other financial professionals they've encountered. They'll realize that you walk the walk, not merely talk the talk about caring about them. They'll realize you made the interaction about them—as it should be, as every client wants it to be.

A final word about listening and feedback before moving on: Can you ever listen and provide too much feedback?

No.

Endnote

1. John D. Rockefeller, Jr., speaking on a radio program sponsored by the United Services Organization, on July 8, 1941, titled as "The Things That Make Life Worth Living." Source: *The World's Great Speeches*, 4th Edition, Dover Publications (1999).

Chapter 5

Any *Simple* Questions?

I will be a fool in question, hoping to be wiser by your answer.
—William Shakespeare, *All's Well That Ends Well*

Whall do you do when the music finally stops? When you sense that your clients have gladly told you everything they thought you should know about their

---

Current situation

Past experiences

Challenges and obstacles

Motivators and drivers

The temptation to move into problem-solving mode is great, but please resist.

Seldom will your clients' stories be complete. Inevitably there will be aspects that are still unclear or undiscovered. You need to probe further. However, now it's your turn to be more direct and ask questions so that no stones are left unturned before you proceed to the next phase of your work on their behalf. The good news is that your clients will be receptive to your inquiries since you were a respectful, encouraging, and empathetic listener.

Some financial professionals apply a Socratic approach to the questioning process. However, when I think of the Socratic approach, I hark back to my days in law school when my Professors "Kingsfield" struck fear and dread in my heart with their unrelenting questioning techniques. While I still suspect at least one or two took great delight in breaking me down, I came to understand that their probing questions were used to help me get to the heart of an important issue and to develop critical thinking skills.

Socratic teaching methods engender critical thinking by asking question after question until exposing contradictions and thereby proving the fallacy of a person's assumptions. I bet your clients can't wait for you to try out some of that on them. For now, let's hold off on the critical thinking element of questioning and concentrate on critical, but simple, questioning skills.

I appreciate the work of well-intentioned experts who have tried to help by publishing books containing extensive lists of questions that financial professionals may use. The books rest on a prominent shelf in my library as a reminder of how smart some people are to be able to recall and use literally hundreds of questions on clients while listening at the same time.

On the other hand, I prefer "KISS" (Keep It Simple, Stupid) because the simpler you keep your critical questioning, the better it will be for you and your clients.

When you ask a question you have two fundamental choices: Go broad or go narrow; explore new fields of interest or seek additional clarification and detail in fields that have already been explored. Use open-ended questions for expansion; use closed-ended questions when you require specificity.

Simple requests or questions such as "Please tell me about..." or "What else should I know" are hybrids that can take open- or closed-ended form depending on how you use them. They take on open-ended meaning when used after your feedback:

> "Mr. Lyon, you have very low regard for consultants who shirk their responsibilities and try to hide behind a lot of consultant-speak, what else should I know?"

and closed-ended meaning when they precede your feedback:

> "Mr. Lyon, please tell me how much the new addition will cost."

"Where," "when," and "who" are close-ended questions, and there's nothing wrong with asking "When and where shall we meet again and who else from your office will be joining us?" But you should guard against turning open-ended inquiries into close-ended questions.

> "Can you tell me what happened next?"

The majority of the time your clients will just tell you what happened next, but given the way the question is phrased, they could say "No," or they might misconstrue the question and think you're doubting their ability to tell you what happened next. Why take a chance when you could just as easily say, "Please tell me what happened next."

Since I just brought up the question "Why," consider the pros and cons of "Why." This is an open-ended question, as are "what" and "how," but your clients could view a "why" inquiry as judgmental or disapproving. See how easy it is, however, to change the tone of the question? Compare "Why did you decide to cancel the policy?" to "Please tell me what led up to the cancellation of the policy." It's a subtle change, but a positive one.

Avoid at all costs multiple questions. Sometimes the questions are related to the same general topic: "What should I know about your retirement plans? How much is in your 401(k), your rollover IRAs, and your Roth IRAs, and how are these accounts invested?"

And at other times multiple questions may come at the client in assorted fronts: "Please tell me where do you do your banking? Have you had wills or trusts prepared? And when do you plan to retire?"

I know "enquiring minds want to know," but you won't advance the relationship by asking multiple questions that confuse and overwhelm your clients.

Another irritating form of question is the *I just thought of a better question than the question I just asked question or was in the process of asking*: "Did they advise you ahead of time...Were you...What reason did they give you for exercising their option?"

You're familiar with the expression, "there's no such thing as a dumb question," but it doesn't apply to financial professionals. The dumbest question you can ask is about something your client just clearly told you, but you weren't listening.

By selecting about a dozen questions to serve as your standards—your "safe harbor" questions—you won't have to use a lot of energy trying to remember or craft all sorts of clever questions, allowing you to expend your energy on a more important activity—listening.

Here are some "safe harbor" questions:

Simple Requests

"Please tell me more."

"Please tell me more about...."

"What else should I know?"

"What else should I know about...?"

"Then what happened?"

"Please continue."

Open-Ended Questions

"What effect will this have on...?"

"How do you feel about...?"

"How important is...?"

"What does ___ think about the situation?"

"What's the purpose of your money?"

"What gives you the greatest satisfaction?"

One additional open-ended question that is frequently used but that merits special consideration is "Please tell me about your goals and objectives."

Because the answer to this question is super-critical, financial professionals must do more than merely ask and listen for the response. You need to help your clients frame their answer in an interactive and collaborative manner.

Some financial professionals will use a deck of specially marked cards that they'll share with their clients. The cards are titled with various goals and objectives for clients to consider and prioritize:

Save for retirement	Plan for income during retirement
Fund educational goals	Pursue a dream or major purchase
Transition a business	Leverage or manage debt
Protect assets	Protect against taxes and inflation
Support parents or children	Define estate and legacy plans
Support charitable causes	Plan for life transitions and unexpected events

These are very personal, thought-provoking, and often emotionally charged financial issues all related to the management of wealth. Your clients will appreciate and value your skillful guidance and counsel as together you reach a mutual understanding of what they want to accomplish and what needs to be done for them to succeed financially.

Your critical listening skills will undoubtedly improve with practice, but they will also improve as you develop or rekindle the skill of note-taking. "Now come on," you're saying to yourself. I paid good money for a book on communication skills, and now I'm told I have to improve my note-taking? What does that have to with building and strengthening client relationships?"

Just about everything.

Not that you ever missed a lot of classes back when you were a student, but on the rare occasion that you did, whose notes did you ask to borrow to catch-up? The smartest kids in the class, of course. But why? Because they were the best note-takers.

When you did the feedback exercise with the Honorable John D. Rockefeller, Jr., did you take notes? If you didn't, do you think taking notes would have helped the quality of your feedback? Probably. Go ahead and try the exercise again, if you want to see for sure.

Note-taking can't help but improve your ability to provide attuned feedback. That's why I've been shocked, on more than a few occasions unfortunately, to be with financial professionals and their clients only to observe a complete dearth of note-taking by my colleagues.

I'll never forget one such incident, after the sudden death of a good friend and colleague. It took place in the offices of his client's attorney and attending the meeting were key members of the client's management, their legal counsel, and their accountant. They graciously convened to meet with the deceased advisor's partner to bring him up to date on the various accounts, to review the communication protocol with the different entities that the client owned throughout the country, and to answer any questions the partner had regarding the continued management and administration of the accounts and what was expected of him. This was fortuitous because the partner had little involvement with the case and knew hardly a thing about the complexities of this very substantial relationship.

What I can't forget is sitting in that conference room for more than an hour and watching a perfectly good pen and perfectly good legal pad go perfectly unused. The partner didn't take a single note. And all I could think about was what were these men and women thinking? Apparently they had nothing noteworthy to say.

Perhaps the partner had some uncanny ability to recall detailed statements and explanations, but I think not, and he never demonstrated that aptitude with any attuned feedback during the meeting. Perhaps he knew that his partner had left instructions on how to handle the relationship in the event he was unable to, but he didn't. Over time—and not a very long period of time— it became evident that the partner simply didn't care. I wasn't surprised to learn the relationship soured and was terminated soon after by the client.

There could be many reasons why that relationship ended. Disappointment with the markets and the performance of the portfolios may have played a major factor. Maybe the partner had no appetite or aptitude for meeting the demands that were placed upon him and his energies would be better spent working with other types of clients. But I wonder if the seeds of that dissolution weren't sown that afternoon when not a note was taken, nor hardly any effort was made on the partner's behalf to show he listened and that he cared.

Capturing Facts and Feelings

When your clients talk to you do they do so in an orderly and organized manner? They may if you attempt to control the flow of information with a formatted questioning process. I favor letting your clients speak their mind without attempting to direct or lead "the witness" like a prosecuting attorney. But when you release the reins what you may hear is a cacophony of free-flowing and random thoughts on a myriad of subjects. And you're expected to provide attuned feedback with facts, feelings, and ideas in the moment.

Take notes. But prepare your notes to make it easier to listen and easier to provide feedback.

Draw a line down the middle of your notes page and on the upper left-hand side write "Facts" and on the upper right-hand side write "Feelings."

You may be surprised as you review your notes to find that most of your recordings are in the "Facts" column—an indication that you are filtering your listening to understand tangible information such as values, performance, and account sizes to the disregard of your client's feelings, emotions, and beliefs.

There are several other ways you can prepare your notes to help you focus and organize what you hear.

Divide your notes page into four boxes and label them "Current Situation," "Past Experiences," "Challenges and Obstacles," and "Motivations and Drivers." Everything you want and need to know about your client will fit into one of these four categories and will help you focus your listening and questioning skills.

Know what you should be listening for; don't listen for what you want to hear.

Know what topics require more attention; don't randomly fire questions at your clients that may or may not hit the mark.

Try adding a few simple reminders to your notes page to help you stay centered on your client and not "go-off" thinking too much and break the connection.

Write down some *simple requests*: "Please tell me more," "What else should I know?" "Then what happened?"

Write down some open-ended question reminders: "What's the status of...?" "What problems are you facing?" "How will that affect you?" or "Why has this come to a boil now?"

Note that the first two questions focus on more factual subjects while the latter two encourage responses that provide insight about feelings and emotions related to urgency, irritants, and causation.

And while you're at it, add two other key reminders to your notes page: a reminder to always begin with a Critical Opener and another to remind you of the four cornerstones of wealth management.

Critical Opener

I'm prepared to discuss... [Think of the four cornerstones of wealth.]

This meeting is about what is most important to you.
Please tell me...

Simple Requests	Open-Ended Questions
Please tell me more [It's so good]	What?
Then what happened?	Why?
What else should I know?	How?

Current Situation	**Past Experiences**

Motivators & Drivers	**Challenges & Obstacles**

Four Cornerstones of Wealth Management

Investments Management	Banking, Credit, and Liability Management
Risk Management	Trust, Estate, and Fiduciary Services

All that on a single sheet of paper? What happens when you run out of room to write?

Yes, yes, you're getting it.

But seriously, it's not just about writing down what your clients are telling you. It's about incorporating the information in your feedback to prove to them that you're listening.

In a mere minute or two, clients may share multiple items of information with you. When they finish, take your time, don't rush, refer to your notes, and deliver your attuned feedback. Then you have a choice: Ask them to expand their remarks generally with a *simple request*—"Please tell me more"—or to expand their remarks specific to one of the points they shared with you and discover all you can about that point with more *simple requests*. When that point has been covered to your satisfaction, refer to your notes and simply request more information about the second, then the third, then the fourth point they brought up. The process is expansive, like a chain letter, but unlike a chain letter, what comes back to you is direct and meaningful and critical to building and solidifying your relationships.

Taking notes in this manner also allows you to provide attuned feedback in a more orderly and organized way. When it's time for you to summarize, you can provide feedback specific to the client's current situation, their past experiences, the obstacles they've shared with you, and what motivates and drives them.

Compare and contrast this approach with a financial professional whose feeble attempts at feedback consist of an occasional "Wow" or "Fantastic" accompanied by a series of questions unrelated to the client's remarks and constructed with a degree of difficulty sure to impress only the inquisitor, not the client.

Inevitably a dialog with a client will stall, perhaps caused by a limiting response to a close-ended question, confusion created by a multiple question, or simply because the client can't think of anything else to say. If you need more information, just relax, look at your notes, and see what areas have not been examined. Then with an open-ended question restart the conversation on a new area of inquiry.

Some Additional Thoughts on Note-Taking

It takes practice, and you're probably out of practice. So don't sweat it. The more you do it the easier it becomes.

But still financial professionals have told me if they take notes they can't maintain eye contact with their clients, and that is important to developing a relationship. I absolutely agree on the importance of eye contact. However, there's one exception: It doesn't matter if you're taking notes. The partner whose colleague passed away maintained great eye contact with everyone in the meeting. But he didn't take notes nor did he offer attuned feedback. Your clients do not need to see your eyes if they see your focus and concentration evidenced by your note-taking.

Make sure you capture unique words or phrases that clients use and in your feedback echo those words or phrases with a simple request to "tell you more."

I remember a prospective client telling a colleague and me that she was looking for a relationship with a firm that "appreciates her business." We both thought that was an unusual sentiment, and we both captured it in our notes and asked her to her tell us more about what she meant by "appreciates your business." What she told us became the core element in our proposal to her months later. We proved to her that we listened to what she told us and that we remembered its significance not just for purposes of our proposal, but throughout our relationship. Would we have remembered and used this had we not taken notes? I don't know. Would it have mattered in the long run? I can only speculate. But I believe little things matter.

There's one more compelling reason to take good notes: It is no longer enough to simply "know your client" and provide full disclosure; it is imperative that you document and be prepared to explain the course of action you recommend along with the basis for your recommendation. And how can you properly document, if you don't take notes?

To wrap up this section on Critical Listening, if you think this whole process is canned or contrived—that it's all a big show, a performance or an act—I respect your opinion. Initially, critical listening will feel unnatural and mechanical until you get the hang of it. And it is a performance, an act; most assuredly it is. It's an act of the deepest commitment, empathy, and respect that you can show your clients. And may all your clients nominate you, in the category of caring, for the Academy Award.

> *It is the province of knowledge to speak and it is the privilege of wisdom to listen.*
> —Oliver Wendell Holmes, Sr., *The Poet at the Breakfast Table*, 1872

Chapter 6

The Secret of Speaking...*Critically*

I never forget a person making a good presentation.
Unfortunately the opposite is also true.
—Jack Welch

Have you ever felt uncomfortable giving a presentation?

(a) Once or twice perhaps.

(b) Several times.

(c) More often than I'd like to admit.

(d) Never, I'm always in command.

If you answered (d), there's no reason for you to read on. You're a liar, but there's no need for you to read on.

For everyone else, which of the following factors may have contributed to your less than optimal performance?

(a) I tried to cover too much material.

(b) I got too technical.

(c) I wasn't technical enough.

(d) I encountered technical difficulties with my presentation.

(e) I didn't follow my plan.

(f) I didn't have a plan to follow.

(g) I was nervous and it showed.

(h) I was too plain, too ordinary, too conventional.

(i) I practiced so much I "left it in the gym."

(j) I didn't practice at all.

(k) I didn't know what to practice.

(l) I'm just not comfortable with public speaking. (I'm better one-on-one.)

If none of these factors ever contributed to your delivery of a disappointing presentation, you're a liar and there's no need for you to read on.

For all you honest, truthful financial professionals still with me, please consider and respond to one more question:

If the "substance" of your presentation constitutes the command of all the facts of the case, the technical subject matter, and the application of wealth management solutions tailored to your clients' needs and objectives; and the "style" of your presentation encompasses how effectively you deliver your advice, counsel, and perspective, which statement most accurately reflects your opinion:

(a) I'm satisfied with my substance but can stand to improve my style.

(b) I'm satisfied with my style but can stand to improve my substance.

(c) There's plenty of room for me to improve both my substance and style.

(d) I am a Master of both substance and style!

If you answered (d), please send me a tape of one of your recent presentations so that I can watch and listen to it in a state of awe and post it on the Internet for all financial professionals to marvel at and admire. For everyone else, please, read on.

I believe whether you're speaking to an individual or a couple in your office, to a committee seated around a conference table, or to a room full of people (clients or otherwise), you're presenting—you're public speaking—and it matters.

You may argue that these venues are very different and they are. You may assert that you're much better, you're more relaxed and more comfortable in personal settings than you are in front of a group of people. You're okay in front of small groups, but because you don't do it every day your presentations are not as "polished" as some, but you think that polished isn't really good if it hides the natural you. And you have such infrequent occasion to speak before larger audiences (or you decline to do so when the opportunity arises) you don't expect that much from yourself, and besides, those settings terrify you.

Unless you're a hermit or a monk who has sworn a vow of silence, you're always presenting, you're always public speaking, whether it's to one individual or one thousand. Every interaction with your clients has a presentation element to it. Whether that element is formal or informal doesn't matter. What matters is how you present yourself. Your regard for your presentation skills in smaller, more intimate settings is simply because you're more at ease in those settings—you're in your comfort zone.

BEWARE.

The comfort zone stifles potential. It's where status quo reigns supreme. The comfort zone impedes professional growth and development. It sucks the life out of once vibrant and vigorous financial professionals. And it's sinister in its ways—slowly, surely, inevitably rendering you a shadow of what you aspire to be. But escape is possible. And once you experience life outside the comfort zone, you'll never turn back.

Breaking out of the comfort zone requires awareness of faults, weaknesses, and your potential for improvement. It requires knowledge of proper techniques that will enhance your presentation skills. It requires practice and a willingness to apply the newly acquired skills for the mutual benefit of you and your clients. And it requires an understanding of what is more important: your substance or your style.

What's More Important?

From your clients' perspectives, what is more important, your substance or your style? I'm sure you're familiar with some form of the Pareto Principle—the 80-20 Rule[1]—one iteration of which suggests that 80%

of your revenue is generated by 20% of your clients. Is it possible that the 80-20 Rule may also be informative for understanding whether your substance or your style has more impact on your clients? And, if so, which is it? Does your substance account for 80% of the impact of your communications? Perhaps it does since "substance," or subject matter expertise has dominated your education and training experiences as well as the majority of your continuing education and professional development initiatives. Is it reasonable to then assert that at least 80% of the impact of your communications is attributable to substance? Or is it somehow the opposite? If style is attributable for 80% of the impact of your communication, then why have you, or your firm, placed so little emphasis on style, or presentation skills throughout your career?

What's the Answer?

The often cited but oversimplified and misinterpreted work of Professor Albert Mehrabian is said to support the hypothesis that 93% percent of the impact of communication is attributable to style, and only 7% is attributable to substance. Style is broken down into two components: Visual, which accounts for 55% of the total impact, and vocal, which accounts for 38%. Again, content only accounts for 7% of the impact of a speaker's communication.

What Mehrabian actually studied was the impact of a speaker's communication on the listener's feelings about the speaker. What causes a listener to feel good about the speaker? What causes a listener to like the speaker?

I've heard financial professionals say countless times, that of all the possible reasons that clients do business with them, the number one reason is because "my clients like me and they trust me."

But what causes them to like you? Or, should we consider what causes them not to like you or feel as good about you as you want them to feel?

Mehrabian believes that people seek out and get involved with things they like, and they try to minimize their relationship or, if possible, entirely avoid contact with things they dislike.[2]

That seems perfectly reasonable and is hard to dispute. But Mehrabian's work tells us that how people feel about you depends on the synchronic consistency of your visual, vocal, and substantive messages. When the alignment of this triad is off, your message will be off.[3] If it's your visual style that throws off your message, that's a big problem. If it's the way you said it, that too is a big problem. And, if there are problems with both your visual and vocal style, you can just forget about it.

Fortunately, however, you shouldn't be too concerned about the substantive aspects of your message since it has far less impact on your clients. You should take solace, as many financial professionals do, in the fact that since you know more about your subject than your clients, at least they can't judge you on the merit of your content.

Hogwash. They're continually judging you on your content. They're continually judging you on everything. Do I sound paranoid? Good, I am and you should be too. What's the title of that book? *Only the Paranoid Survive* by Andrew S. Grove (Doubleday Business, 1996). The title says it all.

But Mehrabian never said content is just "7%" important.

As financial professionals we have a duty to know and skillfully apply our subject matter. I believe it's a fiduciary duty (others may disagree), but whatever duty or standard applies, we have a moral obligation to our clients, to our firm, and to everyone who looks to us for our guidance, counsel, and advice to know our craft and disciplines. Moreover, if we believe in what we do, and that what we do matters, we have a responsibility to get our message across.

How does your message come across?

"I really like Bob Finder because he's so smart, articulate, and handsome."

Wow, thanks, for the compliment. But not so fast, you say. The speaker's message is clear (although two out of the three adjectives are debatable). However, what if the speaker grimaced instead of smiled when speaking those words? What if a tinge of sarcasm was evident in her voice—how she spoke the words "really" and "so"? The visual and vocal aspects of the statement would be received in stark contradiction to (no doubt) the meaning and intent of the statement.

That's why you need to be aware of the visual and vocal idiosyncrasies that create conflict within your message. Such conflicts and inconsistencies can distract your clients and detract from your message and, ultimately, how your clients feel about you.

You may still harbor some doubt about all this, because you have personal experience with plenty of "poor" speakers whom you like, trust, and admire. But the issue is not only about likability, trustworthiness, and admiration; it's about whether you like listening to them speak. If you don't, what are the odds that you'll come away thinking about their message as they hoped and intended you to do? What are the chances you'll take to heart and remember what they said, and more importantly act upon it? And in the process, might you not just begin to wonder why they didn't respect and care more about you? Can you fathom your clients wondering the same?

Are you ready to go outside your comfort zone? I'm not asking you to stop being who you are. I would never think of doing so. Your personal style and attributes have made you who and what you are. No one should ever tamper with that. All I'm suggesting is that you jettison what doesn't add to the impact and effectiveness of your presentation style and try out some skills and techniques that will.

Just do the math:

The sum of all that you do that is positive and effective.

Less: The sum of the distractions and detractions.

Equals: A more compelling and engaging presenter.

Then Add: A few new techniques and skills that will enhance your communication skills.

Result: Power. Transformational power to help your clients succeed financially and for you to achieve further success professionally and personally.

Say "goodbye" to your comfort zone and let's go to work on critical speaking.

Endnotes

1. This is named for the Italian economist Vilfredo Pareto. In 1906, he noted that in his garden, 80% of peas were harvested from 20% of pods. Since then the same idea has been applied broadly in business, sales, client relationships, and elsewhere.

2. Albert Mchrabian, *Silent Messages: Implicit Communication of Emotions and Attitudes*, Wadsworth Publishing, 1981: p. 22.

3. Albert Mehrabian, *Nonverbal Communication*, AldineTransaction, 1971 (5th paperback printing, 2010).

Chapter 7

Just Get Rid of Them

...full of sound and fury, signifying nothing.
—William Shakespeare, *Macbeth*

Whether you're engaged in a casual dialogue with a client or making a presentation to a group, large or small, nothing is more annoying, irritating, and distracting to your audience than the incessant uttering of non-words. Non-words go by many names: "verbal disinfluencies," "oral graffiti," "word parsley," but the latter is disrespectful to parsley for while parsley is not a dietary staple, at least a thoughtful and talented chef may use it to make the presentation of a special dish look good. Unceasing barrages of non-words, however, serve no useful purpose and make your presentations difficult to swallow.

I'm not concerned about the occasional slippage of a non-word. It's unavoidable and no big deal unless you allow non-words to become a big deal. A single ant won't ruin your picnic, but then again, when did you see just a single ant at a picnic?

Non-Words

ah	a little bit	you know
um	basically	as you can see
really	actually	honestly
so	okay	you guys
like	all right	as you know

"Ah," "Um," "And, um" and their undistinguished progeny are nothing more than noise. Purposeless bursts of sound—unpleasant to the ear—and all too predictable. You see them coming before you hear them, and you know more, plenty more, will follow. Linguists may be able to crack the meaning of ancient and dead languages, but they have only been able to hypothesize that these vocal sensations are associated with a lack of preparation, indecision, nervousness, or disregard for others.

"Really" and **"honestly"** are poor attempts to instill candor and truthfulness. The more you use them, the more your client is going to wonder if you're "really" sure what you're saying. And is there any reason clients should expect anything but the truth from you?

"Really" is also used to emphasize a subject or a statement, but the effect is weak.

"What I *really* want to do"

"There are *really* four pillars to wealth management"

"What we *really* do for our clients"

"Our advice model *really* offers"

"We *really* embrace open architecture"

"We *really, really* want to focus on"

In each of the above examples, simply eliminate the word "really" and use vocal inflection for emphasis.

"A little bit" suggests you're not that interested in what your clients have to say or you're holding back. Your intention may be that you don't want to burden your clients with the responsibility to give you a long, lengthy explanation of something, or that you don't want to belabor a point that you want to make, but your intention can be lost in perception—the perception that you're not interested in your clients or the perception that your clients only deserve "a little" of what you have to offer.

"Tell me *a little bit* about yourself."

"Tell me *a little bit* about how you feel."

"Let me tell you *a little bit* about the firm."

"I've done *a little bit* of research."

"I'm a *little bit* concerned."

"I'd like to talk *a little bit* about..."

"As you know," its derivative **"you know,"** and its relative **"as you can see"** are a lazy financial professional's non-words. They are ill-advised phrases that irritate clients because they "don't know," which is the primary reason they're seeking your services. Of course, they are too polite to tell you they "don't know." It's your job to explain what you want them to know in plain, simple English, no technical jargon. Explain exactly what they're looking at when you use handouts or visual aids. Don't say, "As you can see on the chart." They haven't the faintest clue what they're looking at. You forget you're not speaking to other financial professionals who would understand at a glance. This is your chance to be your clients' teacher. They're your eager and willing students. Teach.

"You guys." First of all, if you're going to use this non-word then at least pronounce it correctly. As a native Chicagoan who also spent several years in the Northeast, I can tell you from firsthand exposure the correct pronunciation is "yuz-gize" although "youse gysses" is perfectly acceptable if you're presenting to the Housewives of New Jersey. But if you're not, show respect for your clients and drop it.

I remember as if it happened yesterday, a presentation a colleague and I were making to a board of a national women's service organization. The all-female board consisted of distinguished business leaders, academicians, and philanthropists. My partner stood up to open the presentation and, you guessed it, the first words out of his mouth were "I want to thank you guys for inviting us to meet with you." I was mortified (and not because he mispronounced "you guys"). Can you imagine what our prospective (and never to become) clients thought? But the use or misuse of "you guys" is not about gender. It's about respect for your client—respect for your audience. How can you go wrong with "Ladies..." or "Gentlemen..." or "Ladies and Gentlemen..." or the plural meaning of "you"? You can't.

One caveat I want to make in the interest of matrimonial harmony. My wife is from the South, and she continually reminds me that "y'all" is perfectly acceptable. Who am I to argue?

"Okay?" "All right?" It's a good idea to periodically check-in with your clients to make sure they're on the same page with you. But it can get annoying if these words punctuate virtually every statement or point the speaker makes leaving the client to wonder, "Doesn't he think I'm capable of understanding this?" And therein lies the problem. As a speaker you don't want your clients thinking about hidden meaning and innuendo. You want them focusing on your message.

One more non-word to cover—my non-word— **"So."** When I rush my speech or break eye contact with my audience, "so" just pops out. I'm working like the dickens to eliminate it. Not much more I can say about it, so let's move on [Oops].

Hedge Words

kind of	probably	I'll try
sort of	I think	maybe

Hedge words undermine and erode your credibility. They're what may have soured Mr. Lyon about consultants who, in his opinion never take a position one way or the other on a matter. But why hedge words have become so prevalent in speech is evident. We've become accustomed to speaking as if we're the audio version of the disclosure and disclaimer provisions in our handouts.

Here's a brief excerpt of a presentation I recently sat in on. I've redacted the speaker's perspective and advice, because neither I nor the clients could discern what it was.

> "Clearly, we could probably...is kind of a lot of risk...probably don't think
>
> ...go and buy maybe...you can probably ladder...um, and,
>
> ah, you know...kind of scale back...kind of define that...kind of
>
> you know, a prescriptive model...kind of look at...kind of go
>
> through the process...kind of giving them some tools...kind of

continue along the same path...if you're willing, kind of, to be aggressive

could kind of cool off a little...kind of come along for the ride

probably difficult to play...kind of priced into the market...

Probably really see...kind of go off the cliff."

Fortunately, there was no cliff nearby, for our sake (or the speaker's).

Special Mention Irritants

thing

tweak

if you will

et cetera

the "business"

mixed, misdirectional pronouns

"machine-gunned" words

compound non- and hedge words

jargon

any word or phrase that you overuse

"Thing" is a cheap non-word. It doesn't represent anything specific. It hardly seems worthy of definition, but in fact it means "an entity existing in space and time." That will impress your clients. Don't be surprised, however, if instead they conjure up images of that disembodied hand in *The Addams Family*.

"Tweak" is a wimpy non-word. Financial professionals may advise adjusting, modifying, or rebalancing a client's plans, but tweak? Your clients pay you to "tweak?"

"If you will" is a suffix-like non-word phrase typically attached to the end of a statement for what purpose? Who knows? Your clients won't.

"Et cetera" is the "make your clients do the work" non-word. Why should you take the trouble to give meaningful examples or illustrations to support your message? It's much more fun to see if they can come up with the "miscellaneous unspecified objects" (or "things") that you had in mind, but decided not to share.

"Never ask me about my business." How ridiculous. You love talking about **the business**. But are you in the same business as Don or Michael or Sonny Corleone? I listen with dismay as financial professionals tell clients all the reasons they "got in the business" (not to mention how the word "got" grates on me). Funny, we want to be treated with the same respect as physicians, lawyers, professors, and other professionals, but you don't hear them talking about themselves being in the medicine business, or the law business, or the teaching business.

The frequent **mixed and misdirectional** use of pronouns—singular and plural—can make it challenging for clients to understand who you're talking about and who does what for them. If the point you're making centers around you, don't make vague reference to "they" or "them" without identifying who you're referencing and what roles they play. Substituting "we" or "they" for "I" can be a lame attempt to shift responsibility to someone else.

"Machine-gunned" words can be non-words or parts of ordinary words spouted in uncontrolled, repeated bursts of speech. This non-clinical stuttering— "Ah, ah, ah, ah," "Le-, le-, le-gacy planning," or "We, we, we, we think"—is caused by the hurried pace of the financial professional's speech and can be eliminated by simply slowing down.

Compound non- and hedge words are total credibility and confidence busters.

"It's probably like"

"I think we believe"

"Clearly, we sort of can"

"Really, probably the biggest thing we need to consider"

"...kind of, a little bit"

"You know, I think we can sort of"

Like, need I kind of say more, okay?

In your core/universal value proposition you promise your clients that you'll explain the wealth management solutions that you've developed for them "in plain, simple English, **no technical jargon.**" So [Oops], keep your word and drop the "efficient frontiers" [never forget the Lyon]; the "HELOC" [Did he just tell me where I can go?]; the "ILIT" [Did she say eye-lid? What's that have to do with protecting our wealth?]; the "UPIA" [That's what we say to our semi-house-broken Jack Russell Terrier]; or I'm a CFP. [Are your clients supposed to know what that means?]

Any word or phrase that you overuse can become a non-word. I was making a presentation once and to emphasize my point I used the phrase, "I submit." I liked the sound of it. It made me feel quite the authority, so, [Oops] I kept using it and using it. Upon reflecting back to that presentation, I must submit, it sucked.

Chapter 8

What Did He Say?

Speak up.
—Anonymous

Now you're talkin'.
—Anonymous

You're aware that America is getting older, and your clients are getting older. With advancing age, hearing naturally begins to deteriorate. It's estimated that one-third of the people in the United States between the ages of 65 and 75 have some degree of hearing loss, and the percentages only increase from there. But to think that hearing loss might not be an issue for your younger clients is a mistake. The majority of people in this country with hearing loss are younger than age 65.[1]

In a typical office or conference room setting with an individual and their spouse, being heard isn't a problem. If your clients can't hear you, they'll just matter-of-factly ask you to speak up. But what if your clients aren't seated directly in front of you? What if you're speaking to a group of people seated around a large conference room table? Or what if you're speaking to a room full of people delivering a seminar or a talk or simply introducing a colleague or the next speaker? Will you be heard [and I don't mean will they listen to you]?

Financial professionals tend not to be a shy and reserved lot, yet surprisingly many are very soft-spoken. When told they need to speak louder, the consensus response is "Louder? Are you kidding? I thought I was screaming." I won't go into the physiological reasons why we think we speak louder than we do, because we can't do much about that except to be aware of the phenomenon. However, you need to be aware of a number of contributing factors to low volume that you can affect.

Lack of energy (tiredness)	Lack of interest in your subject	
Time of day	Size	Ambient noise
Unsustainable pace	Coasting across the finish line	Lack of eye contact

Toward the end of a long and demanding day, when you're tired and your energy level is down, it's difficult to perform any skill or activity well, and speaking is no exception. But sometimes what you're tired of is the sound of your own voice because you've been talking too much and too long and as a result, your energy is dissipating. When your energy drops, volume drops and so does interest—yours and your client's.

The "same-old-same-old" talk or conversation gets stale quickly. And when it does, your energy level drops with a corresponding decrease in your volume. When you sense that's happening, think creatively and find new ways to express your subject matter. You'll experience a spike in your energy and enthusiasm and with it, the volume of your speech.

Be aware of ambient noise that you need to compete against. Sometimes it's an easy win—just close a door or turn off the TV. "Daah," you're thinking, but how many times have you thought it unnecessary? Do you adjust your volume to compete against the constant buzz of a projector or the intermittent hissing from the AC or heating system? And what do you do about "thin walls with noisy neighbors?"

A colleague recently invited me to attend a dinner seminar he was sponsoring at a classy restaurant that just happened to be one of my favorites. He told me he'd like me to critique the event. I think he also wants my account (but the former is sure worth a lot more than the latter). I've been to a number of such functions at this establishment held in the same room as we were in that evening, and it had always been a fine setting for good food and good conversation, but not that evening. I never found out who those people were in the adjacent dining room, but one thing was for sure—they were having a helluva good time. I felt bad for my colleague. I felt worse for his guests. It was extremely difficult to hear what he had to say, and as (bad) luck would have it, when the roar from the other room abated for a few minutes, my friend still had to compete with the noise and ruckus of the wait staff within our room.

Oh, as for my critique and suggestions:

The seminar was way too long—total time 2 3/4 hours with 45 minutes of presentation time.

It was too PowerPoint-dependent—47 slides, and he went through every one.

Parts of it were corny and clearly developed by marketing types who have never been in front of real clients or prospects.

And NEVER speak while your guests are eating. Putting myself in the mindset of the guests and prospective clients (which perhaps I was), I felt guilty. "Guilty of what?" you may be thinking. Guilty of eating my dinner while he was speaking. And as I looked around at the other guests, I sensed that many of them were conflicted and felt the same way, having divided allegiance to our host and to either the sizzling Prime New York Strip steak or fresh Copper River salmon cooked over white hot coals and Alderwood. Tough position to put your guests in: steak or salmon (or listening to you).

Noticeable decreases in volume tend to come toward the end of long statements and long presentations. The former is caused when presenters speak in run-on-sentences, delivering one thought or idea after another and another and another and another droning on and on and on and on until finally literally, figuratively, and physiologically running out of breath they reach a critical juncture and must decide whether to pause and come up for air or continue undeterred by light-headedness and the prospect of passing out.

Hopefully, they will not ask their audience's opinion.

Or, with the end of their presentation in sight, some financial professionals coast across the finish line, pulling back like a horse that's been beaten, satisfied to merely finish and race another day. Instead of finishing with a crescendo, they finish with a whimper.

Your eyes can also affect your volume. If you speak to your notes instead of to your clients, your volume is projected downward not outward. If you turn away from your audience and speak to a screen or flip chart—besides being inexcusable—your volume level crashes (at least from the audience's perception, but the screen or flip chart will hear you just fine).

Your eyes may also be a catalyst for your dreaded non-words and hedge words. I'll have more to say about that in the next chapter.

Size affects volume too. Not just the size of the room or the table around which you and your clients are seated, your physical size matters particularly if you're a man or woman of stature. Many financial professionals I know come to mind, but one in particular who literally stands out is a tall, rugged, well-built gentleman, whom if I didn't know better, could be "The Most Interesting Man in the World." All eyes gravitate to him whenever he enters a room, but when he speaks, he sounds like a mouse. And it's not because he doesn't have a strong voice. He does. But he's afraid to "play big." If you're big, play big, play to your strength. Don't overpower your audience with your voice, but don't disappoint them either. Surprise them—engage them with the richness and range of your voice. But if you're small or petite, don't "play small." Develop and play the full range of your voice. Get out of your comfort zone.

Your volume may be perfectly suited for the environment in which you work and meet with clients. But can you control your environment away from your office—at your client's home or office or at that noisy restaurant where you're hosting a seminar? If you were a professional place-kicker instead of a financial professional, I know you'd be able to kick a P.A.T. or a 25-yard field goal with no problem. But if I was the General Manager, considering signing you to a lucrative multi-year contract, wouldn't I want to see how you fared at 45-, 50-, 55- even 60-yards? I sure hope you wouldn't be called on too frequently to win a game with a 60-yarder, but if the team needed it, it would be good to know you had the range.

Volume lets you be heard. Your tone of voice lets your feelings be known.

Think of your clients; think of your audience. You want them to like you. Will making them endure your dull, drab, boring, inflectionless, monotone manner of speaking help your cause? It might be tolerable if you're the smartest, best-trained, and most skillful financial professional in your community—you're *numero uno*; you're without peers; you're "the" go-to person. If the demand for your advice and counsel is so high that clients are willing to pay any price, monetarily or otherwise, to retain your services, what does it matter how you sound when you speak? It won't. But if you're not *numero uno*, if your speech is not dynamic, if your tone of voice is mundane, you need to make some changes.

You should sound—whether one-on-one with a prospect or in front of a room full of people—like you are hosting a dinner party for dear friends and special guests. Your voice should speak volumes (in all ranges) of your enthusiasm and your confidence; of your passion and thoughtfulness; of your concern and consideration for your dear friends and special guests. And something else will happen when you find your voice—your nervousness will abate for you are among friends.

The last words on the words you speak: SLOW DOWN. Financial professionals speak too fast. You're addressing an array of delicate subjects and complex issues that can't be—shouldn't be—rushed. While you may be comfortable with the brisk pace of your speech, your clients won't be. Do you want them to think you're rushing because you have more important things to do? Do you think they'll be able to digest and process all the information you're delivering at the same pace that you're able to with all your years of experience and training?

It's okay to PAUSE. In fact, you have to. Silence is golden. It allows your clients to absorb what they've heard, and it allows you time to center yourself and make any midcourse adjustments that are necessary. Stop shooting from the hip, guns-a-blazin'. You could get lucky and hit your target, but more likely, you'll miss (and your clients will miss out on what could have made a big difference in their financial lives).

Endnote

1. Sergei Kochkin, Ph.D., "Prevalence of Hearing Loss," Better Hearing Institute; "Hearing Loss," Mayo Clinic Staff, 2011.

Chapter 9

The Eyes Say It All

Seeing is believing.
—Anonymous

How do you feel when someone is talking to you, but they just can't seem to look you in the eyes?

They may occasionally glance at you, but for the most part their face angles to the side or down and away from you. These folks remind me of my dogs, Peabody and Sherman, only in reverse. When they want something—a treat, to play, or to go out to do their business—they look me straight in the eyes and bark. But try to give them a command, "Look over here, Sherman. Come on, Sherman, this way, over here," so [Oops] I can snap a picture because he looks so [Oops] cute chewing up Ginger's only pair of Gucci shoes, what does he do? He looks in every direction except mine as if I wasn't there. How does it make you feel when people look in every direction except yours when they're speaking to you?

How do you feel when you're in the audience and the speaker is reading his speech? Not referencing his notes, I mean reading the text word for word. Do the intermittent attempts to make contact with the audience by looking up make you feel better about the speaker— more engaged and connected to him? Or what about the presenter who may not be reading his speech verbatim but is so note-dependent that he'll need an appointment with a good chiropractor to get the kinks out of his neck because of all the bobbing up-and-down to his notes—to the audience—to his notes—to his clients—to his notes? How does that make you feel? And how do you feel when that note-dependent presenter has to refer to his notes as he delivers his opening remarks; as he tells you about himself and his team; as he relates a personal and moving experience; or as he leaves you with his closing thoughts? How do you feel?

The word may be mightier than the sword, but spoken words must be seen to be believed.

The Significance of the Eyes:

Keep your eye on the ball.

Do we see eye-to-eye?

Eye of the tiger.

Beauty is in the eye of the beholder.

I only have eyes for you.

> The eyes of Texas are upon you.
>
> The eyes tell all.
>
> The eyes are the window to the soul.
>
> Eye-opening experience
>
> Don't fire until you see the whites of their eyes.

These familiar expressions, idioms, and statements all relate to the power of your eyes—all except the last. "Don't fire until you see the whites of their eyes" has been attributed to many military leaders over the centuries who wisely instructed their forces to hold their fire until the most opportune time. Yet, this direction will have profound effect on your ability to connect with your clients by replacing the word "fire" with the word "speak."

Your battle cry should always be: Don't speak until you see the sclera—the whites of your clients' eyes.

I'm not too concerned about your eye contact in one-on-one settings with your clients because I know you neither ignore them nor stare them down when you're speaking. However, when you add more clients or more people to the mix, how would you characterize your eye contact?

Do you dart from one person to the next afraid of focusing on anyone for fear that Medusa is lurking within your present company?

Do you sweep the room glancing briefly at each person like the beacon from a lighthouse rotating left, then right, then back again left and then back again right?

Do you speak over your clients' heads, literally (and figuratively)?

Do you speak exclusively to the decision-makers, such as the head of the investment committee or to the head of the household (always the husband, *of course*)?

Do you turn your back to your clients and read your PowerPoint slides—all the slides and everything on the slides but apologizing because you know your clients can't read the slides for themselves because (a) they can't read or (b) the slides are illegible?

Do you gaze down at your notes to get a head start on the next point in your presentation as you're still explaining the point you're trying to make?

All of these habits are common, all of them are bad, and all of them can be broken. Here's how:

1. Don't speak—I mean it. Don't say a single word until you're looking directly at your client or a member of the audience and see the whites of their eyes.

   But what if the person you randomly choose to speak to isn't looking directly back at you? Don't let it worry or bother you. That's going to happen. Your clients or audience won't always be fixated on you. You never know when they'll be texting, checking messages, or otherwise temporarily distracted. Some may be talking on the phone or talking to another audience member or they could be playing Sudoku, knitting, or sleeping (hopefully not your fault, but we'll get to that issue later).

2. Pretend. Whenever your clients or audience aren't looking at you simply pretend they are by visualizing a wide-open, interested, and **impressionistic** pair of eyes looking right back at you even if you have to place those "eyes" on the top of someone's head. And remember, you still haven't uttered a word or a sound.

   Now you're ready to speak and speak as you do in the comfort of your office to your dearest client. Your objective is to reach and connect with your clients—one at a time not *en masse*. You'll also notice an interesting phenomenon occurs when you make the connection with one client, and then with another and another—they feed off of your energy and the positive feelings emanating throughout the room—all for one and one for all. Then—

3. FINISH. Complete your thought or idea on the single client whom you have engaged with your eyes. Don't begin your point on one client and finish on another or several others. What constitutes your "point" may require several sentences to convey the proper meaning or it may consist of a single word.

Imagine speaking the following words as you scan a group of clients with no direct eye engagement:

"My advice is independent, objective and unbiased."

Great concept, but will it stick?

Now consider the impact of making the same statement, but delivering the three distinct elements of your statement to three separate clients:

Engaging Client A—"My advice is independent, (pause)

Engaging Client B—objective (pause)

Engaging Client C—and unbiased."

Or, consider the impact of delivering three distinct, but related statements to three separate clients instead of just one:

Engaging Client A—"My advice is independent, objective and unbiased." (pause)

Engaging Client B—"Controlling costs and expenses is always a key consideration of the wealth management solutions that I propose." (pause)

Engaging Client C—"And I will present and explain my recommendations in plain simple English, no technical jargon."

I have no doubt that with your eye engagement, along with the proper tone and inflection of your voice, these words will connect with Clients A, B, and C as well as with any other clients seated around them.

How should you sit in relation to your clients? While I know you "sit on the same side of the table" as your clients, physically speaking you most likely don't. Most of the time you spend with your clients, you're seated across a desk from them, at a small round conference table, or perhaps at a larger boardroom table. Is there a "right" or a "wrong" way to sit in these settings? Or should you be seated?

I'd like you to try something. If you're sitting down at a desk or table, place your arms in your lap or casually let them hang at your sides. Don't worry for now about the slouch in your posture, just consider how you look? More importantly how do you think your clients would feel looking at you?

Of course, you haven't been doing anything improper sitting there like that, but just to be safe, like the cops say on TV, "Put your hands where I can see them," and as your mother always told you, "sit up straight." Now consider how you look and how your clients would feel. Better.

Good, your hands are on the table, now put the pen down—unless you're taking notes. Pens are instruments for writing, not toys or objects to fidget with, tap, click, point, or doodle with. And don't substitute your reading glasses for the pen. Reading glasses help you read; they serve no constructive purpose when you're fidgeting with them.

And who said you have to remain seated at all times? How about getting off your keister once in a while to change the dynamics of the meeting? When an opportunity presents itself to step up to a whiteboard, flip chart, or projection screen to explain a point, take it. Make it an "event," a teaching experience, something your clients will appreciate you doing for them, something they'll remember. However, don't forget, if you're illustrating something on the whiteboard or explaining a slide projected on the screen, "don't speak until you see the sclera."

Suppose now, that you're making a presentation in a venue that you're unfamiliar with or can't control, and you're seated at a large conference room table in one of those nice ergonomic adjustable chairs except the height adjustment mechanism is broken. It's set on the lowest level, and it's the only chair available. You realize your head and just about five or six inches of your neck and torso are above the table, and you feel like a small child in a grown-up world. What do you when it's your time to present? Stand.

If you're presenting in a more formal setting, you may have little option but to stand, but this may not exactly be your strong suit. All eyes are on you and you can feel them. You're outside your comfort zone. You're nervous and they can sense it. What's giving it away?

Wardrobe malfunction, perhaps? Why else would your hands be substituting for fig leafs?

Playing with a miniature percussion section in your pocket? It sounds like that with you jingling all those coins and keys. And if you're not fiddling with all that change, then what are you doing in there? Don't forget, put your hands where your clients can see them.

Are you expecting that at any time, someone may throw you a watermelon? Elbows against your sides, forearms extended, hands at approximately 305° and 45°. Looks like the watermelon-catching ready position to your clients.

What are you doing with the pen or marker? You never use it to write. Obviously it's serving no purpose unless your purpose is to distract your clients.

Is everything all right at home? Look how your wedding band spins.

Are your hands magnetized? They're clasped together tighter than a bank's lending standards. And watch the struggle as you try to break the force, but all that wringing only makes the force grow stronger. And then watch how every so often...there...that big thumb flicks. Must be some sort of signal for help.

Are you giving your clients the finger—the index finger?

Do you think you might lose your balance? Is that why you're holding onto or touching the table? Watch out, some tables tend to have a touch of glue on the surface and you might never lift your hands off, or a loose leg can send you and the table crashing, slapstick-style, to the floor, and that's all they'll remember about you.

Are you trying to light a fire or do you always rub your left thumb and index finger together like that?

Enough. I apologize. I know this all sounds ridiculous. But does it happen? Unfortunately, all too frequently and not just to rookie financial professionals.

Here's what you should do with your arms and hands: A few minutes before your presentation, "warm up." Shake it out, loosen up, extend and roll your arms, wiggle your fingers, do a few jumping jacks (minus the jumping). Thirty to sixty seconds will suffice. No need to break a sweat though; that will come naturally.

Now relax your shoulders and let your arms hang naturally by your sides. Try it.

"Naturally?" you're thinking. "This guy has to be kidding. That feels awful."

I don't care how you feel. I care how your clients and your audience feel. Granted, no one will ever retain your services because they like how you keep your hands at your sides, but don't keep expecting them to throw you a watermelon either.

Let's call arms-at-your-side your base position. From this base you want to move your arms and hands to bring energy to your presentation, amplify your message, and connect with your clients.

Remember the tall, rugged, well-built financial professional I mentioned earlier—the one who could stand in for "The Most Interesting Man in the World" but for his mousy voice? Now imagine that he's raised his volume, he's speaking with more inflection, and he's varying the pace of his speech to fit his message. Big improvements, but he's standing there with those watermelon-catching arms. He's still playing small. What can he do?

From the base position, he can engage his client by extending the arm nearest to the client in the client's direction and with an open hand. In essence, his arm and hand leads his eyes to the client and they connect. His extended arm has about 5° of bend at the elbow to release the tension and to keep him from looking stiff. His other arm is relaxed at his side in the base position. When he completes his point with the client, he engages another client repeating the process, with his right hand or left, it doesn't matter. It's not a mechanical, predetermined routine. It's an option that he and you will get comfortable with with practice, and that you will use to engage and connect with your clients.

You also want to practice gesturing to animate and emphasize key points in your speech. This comes easily for me because I'm Italian—Finder, of course, that's Italian. No, really, both of my maternal grandparents were from Italy, but enough about my family lineage. The point I want to make is that I've been told I talk a lot with my hands. That's fine in business and social conversations as long as the gestures are purposeful and not merely gestures for the sake of movement. [Of course in social settings I think my gestures are purposeful; Ginger thinks they're just downright annoying.]

She may be right [May?] but in a business setting with a client, if I'm explaining, "That as interests rise, bond prices will fall" this would be an opportune time to raise my hand in sync with "as interest rates rise" and lower my hand as "bond prices fall." Simple. Try it.

No. Bigger. Bigger. Stop playing small.

Now try gesturing as you're explaining, "Comprehensive wealth is more than investments. Think of comprehensive wealth as consisting of four cornerstones."

That's right, you drew a box with your gesture (although it needs to be bigger because you're describing comprehensive wealth management, not teeny-weeny wealth management).

Then as you describe each of the cornerstones of wealth, you punctuate them with a gesture as if you're placing "banking, credit, lending, and liability management" in its cornerstone; then risk management; trust, estate, and fiduciary services; and investments in their respective cornerstones.

Purposeful gesturing adds energy to your speech. Do you remember listening to and watching a monotone speaker who effectively gestured? Of course you don't. No one does, except for the wrong reasons.

There's one type of gesture that is almost always in sync with the spoken words, but I find unimpressive: counting on your fingers. Imagine the Most Interesting Financial Professional in the World explaining that "We have a five-step process: Step one (this little piggy went to market); step two (this little piggy stayed home); step three (this little piggy had roast beef); step four (this little piggy had none); and step five (this little piggy went wee wee all the way home)."

Come on, you can play and gesture bigger and better than that. And besides, isn't it embarrassing when you hold up four fingers to signify your five-step process?

While purposeful gestures enhance your speech, also be aware of your positioning in relation to your clients or audience especially in larger venues with more spacious settings. You may think you're developing closer connections with your clients by physically moving from one side of the room to the other, but as you connect with some are you turning your shoulder or worse, your back, on others? You can just as easily connect with anyone in the room with the simple turn of your head and extension of your arms to your clients seated, in theatrical parlance, front-stage right; back-stage right; back-stage left; front-stage left; and anywhere in between.

If you're using visual aids, don't block your clients' line of sight, or if you're using a front-lit projector, don't stand in the light with text, graphs, or pictures prominently displayed on you instead of on the screen. Funny thing is, you won't even think you're doing it, but your clients will.

Something you may not realize you're doing when delivering a standing presentation is rocking side-to-side, swaying back-and-forth or moving forward toward your clients and then backing away and genu flecting.

Yes, genuflecting. No one commanded the stage like one of my long-time associates. When he spoke to his clients they were spellbound. Not by his message, but by the repeated knee bends that occurred throughout his presentations. It was so noticeable (to everyone but him) that you could hear whispers in the audience, wagers being made, big money changing hands: "I think he's going to do it...now! Yeah, I win, told you so, pay up."

Because this man is truly one of the good guys in our profession, I asked him if I could videotape his next presentation and he agreed. When he watched his tape, he laughed and said, "Why the heck do I keep doing that? I look ridiculous." The truth of the matter is that he didn't look ridiculous—not when he was in the batter's box back in college facing a pitcher with a wicked curve ball and mean change-up both complementing a smoking fastball. Flexing his knees was a natural response mechanism to release the nervous energy building up. It helped him relax. He finished his college with a career batting average of .285—pretty darn respectable, not major league potential, but pretty darn respectable and coincidentally, just about his "close ratio" for winning new wealth management relationships, again pretty darn respectable. But do you think he was satisfied? Today, his closing average has improved significantly and more importantly, his clients see him as a hall of famer, but they'll never see him genuflecting.

> *Smile and the world smiles with you. Frown and the world frowns upon you.*
> —Verlin B. Hinsz and Judith A. Tomhave, *Personality and Social Psychology Bulletin*, October, 1991

If the wrong visual cues and facial expressions impair the message you're delivering to your clients, what difference will smiling make?

All the difference in the world.

Now please go look in a mirror and smile. Not a Cheshire Cat grin, your normal, natural smile.

Don't be afraid to use it. You can create the best wealth management solutions ever developed for your clients using all your education and training; all your experience and judgment; and all your resources and resourcefulness. But be sure to let that warm smile show your clients that you care and understand, and that they're going to be okay.

Dress with Respect

> *Mirror, mirror on the wall...*
> —Jacob and Wilhelm Grimm, *Snow White and the Seven Dwarfs*, 1812

I once gave a presentation to a group of financial professionals, and it was one of those special times when everything went flawlessly. My message was compelling, my delivery inspirational, and I knew I captured the hearts and minds of my audience. Afterward a gentleman approached me and asked "Where do you get your material?" With great pride I explained my research protocols and discussions with various experts in our industry who helped me formulate my opinions. But then he interrupted me, "No, I mean where do you get your material? I really like that fabric."

If Mehrabian is right (and I believe he is), the way you look in all of its facets affects the way people feel about you. One facet I haven't addressed until now is to what extent does your wardrobe contribute to positive or negative client perceptions of you? I recognize the sensitivity of this subject and the thin ice I'm on with this topic. I have no desire to become the financial industry's Mr. Blackwell; however, I can't help but notice that many financial professionals have very little regard for the way they dress. They couldn't care less and they don't think it matters to their clients.

What do you think is wrong, if anything, with a colleague of mine wearing a sport coat to a prospective client's office to discuss the client's interest in changing his banking and investment relationship? While my colleague and the owners of the business weren't close friends, they did know one another through their involvement in various civic organizations and enjoyed what could be regarded as cordial relations.

What I forgot to mention was that he was also wearing one of those cheap ties with the little chili peppers and bottles of that spicy condiment all over of it.

Did you just grimace? Why? Don't you like Tabasco ties?

I know another financial professional who, on his way to the club for his regular Saturday morning match, stopped by a client's home to drop off some reports the client had requested. I thought this was a nice example of those little client-service "extras" that come instinctively for many financial professionals, but later I learned that his client was offended when he entered his home wearing tennis attire.

If you think this client was over the line, I understand, but is that what matters? Who needs (or wants) a client like this? Life's too short you may be thinking.

Would you feel differently if I told you the annual fees from that relationship were very substantial? Probably not. But what if I told you that the financial professional knew that for more than thirty years, this client spent every Saturday morning at his plant working on ways to grow and strengthen his business? Unfortunately, that financial professional lost that relationship not long thereafter for reasons never clearly understood. [Are they ever?]

What's the morale of these two stories? Never wear a cheap tie to a business meeting—correction, never wear cheap ties—and always think about your client's perception.

Dress with respect for yourself and your client. When you look good, you feel good. You carry yourself differently; you walk taller and with more confidence, Dressing well shows that you care about yourself and your clients (and your colleagues, friends, and family).

Finder's Fashion Suggestions

Wear "classic" clothing styles instead of short-lived fashion fads and trends.

Sharp ties and scarves add "pop."

No "bling."

You can always dress-down, but not vice-versa.

Get a good tailor or seamstress; go on a diet; or both.

Chapter 10

Are You a Substance Abuser?

Stop financial substance abuse.
—Yours truly

I hear comments all the time from financial professionals that they hate practicing their presentations in
front of colleagues because those colleagues can
always tell if you know your stuff. That's reasonable.
You're out of your comfort zone practicing in front of
colleagues because you do it so infrequently, if at all.
However, when you're with clients—when you're in
your comfort zone—you're not as concerned. Why?
Because your clients won't be able to tell as easily if you
don't know your stuff, and besides, substance is attributable for only 7% of the impact of your communications.

Wrong, on both counts. Clients can tell and subject
matter matters. Your clients look to you for your subject matter expertise. They rely on it and you owe it
them. I take it as a given that you know your substance;
what I'm concerned about is whether you're a habitual
financial substance abuser.

Einstein may have described you as an "intelligent fool" because of your tendency to "make things bigger and more complex" than they are, but he also held up hope that with "a touch of genius" and "a lot of courage" it's possible to move in the right direction.[1]

Stop trying to cover the waterfront of technical subjects with your clients or diving into the minutia because you think that's how you establish professional credibility. In most cases, it's unnecessary.

Think about your practice and the types of clients you work with—the majority of your discussions center around a few key, recurring subjects. You should focus on those core, fundamental subjects and make sure you're explaining them in a concise, clear, and compelling manner, instead of

- Oversimplifying—Speaking down to your client

- Overcomplicating—Speaking over their heads

- Overwhelming—Speaking in unnecessary levels of detail

Your mastery of these recurring subjects are your *safe harbors*—explanations that reduce or eliminate unnecessary information and filler. "Filler" and its companion "fluff" serve no purpose unless you want to come across as unprepared and superficial. *Safe harbors* enable you to filter out excess and nonessential information and streamline your presentation—boiling it down to the essence.

By listening critically to your clients, you will be able to determine which *safe harbors* to use instead of drifting about aimlessly in vast seas of too much or too little information.

While *safe harbor* subjects differ from practice to practice, one applies to all financial professionals and that's your core/universal value proposition. Moreover, each of its four elements constitutes a separate safe harbor that can be used independent of the others.

For example, if a prospective client—a high net worth individual or an institution—says, "Please tell me about your process," the third element of your core/universal value proposition is your ready, *safe harbor* response:

Listen and understand.

Analyze and develop solutions.

Explain your recommendations in plain English.

Implement solutions in an independent, objective, unbiased, and cost-effective manner.

Monitor, evaluate, and adjust.

The benefit of drawing on *safe harbors* is that you're not continually reinventing the wheel. This enables you to tie critical facts, feelings, and emotions that you've discovered about your client to your explanation, thus making it relevant. Your message is either relevant or irrelevant. If it's the former, it moves the relationship forward, but if it's the latter, the relationship may stall or even worse, die. Consider how this financial professional incorporated his client's emotions (frustration and doubt) and state-of-mind (one-sided relationship) into a description of the beginning phase of his wealth management process:

"Your frustration with your current advisor is understandable. When a relationship is one-sided as you've described it has to be cause for concern. You should know that **my process** always **begins** and ends **by listening** to my clients. It's critical that I have an in-depth understanding not only of your current situation, but also how past experiences come into play, and of course, what you want to do with your money moving forward."

You don't have to come up with a new way to explain your process whenever the subject arises. All you have to do is tie what you know about your client to the key elements of your safe harbor.

Play it safe.
—Anonymous

Wherever your clients reside, Missouri or elsewhere, they expect you to be able to support the sum and substance of your position. You can do so by playing it *safe* or by playing it *safe*.

Statistics	**S**afe harbors
Analytics	**A**nalogies
Facts	**F**eelings
Experts	**E**xperiences

To explain:

Some financial professionals support their position by playing it safe using statistics, analytics, facts, and expert references. If used properly these evidentiary tools help you establish credibility with your clients; if overused or used improperly they do the opposite.

Statistics, Analytics, and Facts

No financial relationship receives more attention than the one between risk and return, but you can't begin to understand return without understanding the role that risk plays in generating it. Within investments—one of the four cornerstones of wealth—risk is often defined as volatility, and one way to measure this is with statistical probability, or standard deviation. I know with almost a 100% statistical probability what you're thinking right now: "Come on, I know all this stuff, get to something I don't know." Granted you do, but what I'm concerned about is whether your clients understand it, and that will depend on (a) whether they took and passed a statistics class, or (b) whether you have explained it to them properly. I think (b) bears further consideration.

The technical description of standard deviation is:

Risk may be regarded as the volatility of returns as measured by the standard deviation of returns, a statistical measure of the variability of a security's returns. Given a statistically significant sample (basically having sufficient data to produce a normal distribution), standard deviation describes the range of historical returns relative to the historical average return and, by inference, the probability of a future possible return relative to the expected (future return). By definition, one standard deviation around the average return will capture approximately 68% of the returns. Similarly, two standard deviations around the average will capture 95% of the returns.

Do you use that on your clients? Probably not, but I bet you use one of these—a scattergram (see Figure 10.1).

I'm also sure that it doesn't take you more than a few seconds to look at the analysis and get an excellent understanding of what it reveals. The problem is, do you take much more than a few seconds to explain it to your clients? Or do you say something like

"As you can see from this scattergram, Top Notch has had very poor performance and has taken on a lot of risk. Risky Business, on the other hand as you can see, takes on a lot of risk, but has performed much better. Now, you know if you want a more conservative manager you should think about Slow and Steady."

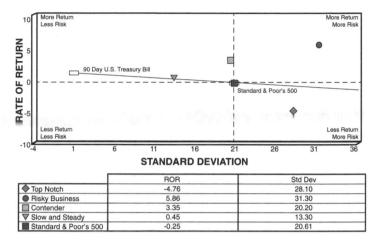

FIGURE 10.1   *Risk/reward analysis.*

Presenting this to a group of your fellow financial professionals is no problem, or is it? Remember how you said you don't like presenting to your peers and colleagues because they'll know what you don't know? But giving you the benefit of the doubt, is there any doubt that such an explanation could still leave plenty of doubt in the minds of your clients?

Anytime you use technical financial materials with a client, regardless of how elementary you find the materials, take your time and explain it to them thoroughly. In the example below, I've inserted superscripted letters indicating an opportunity for you to incorporate gestures in your explanation if you were projecting the analytics on a screen. A gesture key follows the text for your consideration.

"I've prepared for your benefit[a] a risk/reward analysis for a five-year period so that we can gain a better understanding of the risk and return characteristics of Top Notch, a money manager recommended by a friend of yours, and Risky Business, a manager that you've been reading a lot about in the papers lately.

The vertical axis measures return[b] and the horizontal axis measures standard deviation.[c] Standard deviation is a measure of risk—the volatility or swings[d] in performance both positive and negative measured from the average return generated by the manager over a specified period of time, again, in this instance five years.

In the cross-hairs[e] of this analysis, I've plotted the S&P 500 Index. It's a commonly used benchmark that helps us gauge the performance of the large cap U.S. equity market and helps us compare the performance of managers like Top Notch and Risky Business to a passively managed index.

From the position of your manager, Top Notch, represented by the diamond in the lower right-hand portion of the diagram,[f] relative to the S&P 500, has underperformed and done so with much higher volatility. I can understand why you're concerned about this manager.[g]

Now look at the position of the circle.[h] It represents Risky Business. It has clearly outperformed Top Notch and the S&P 500 over this period of time although it is even slightly more volatile than Top Notch—see how it is farther to the right[i] along the volatility or risk scale.

Gesture Key

a—Standing to the left of the projected slide (because clients read from left to right and you want them "returning" to you because this is about you not the slide—the slide is only a visual aid) point with an extended left arm in the direction of the title of the slide.

b—Make a gradual up-and-down gesture indicating the vertical axis; and

c—A long sideways gesture indicating the horizontal axis.

d—With your right arm, give a pronounced and repeated up-and-down gesture that suggests the gyrations that constitute volatility.

e—"Draw" the cross-hairs with an up-and-down and sideways gesture.

f—With your left arm direct your clients' eyes to the lower right-hand portion of the slide.

g—Use a watermelon-arms-like gesture, with both hands turned out about 45°, to express your empathy.

h—Angle your left arm toward the upward right-hand portion of the slide in the direction of the circle representing Risky Business.

i—With your left arm, "push" your clients' attention to the left toward the higher volatility range of the slide.

What do you think—a credible explanation of the risk/reward analysis that you're presenting to your client? Not bad, and what did it take, at most 2 minutes to explain. But did your explanation convey the magnitude of the inferred potential risk of, let's say, Risky Business? What could you do to make your explanation more provocative?

Consider doing the math for your client. On a flip chart or legal pad, take the data from the illustration and demonstrate what it means, as shown in Figure 10.2.

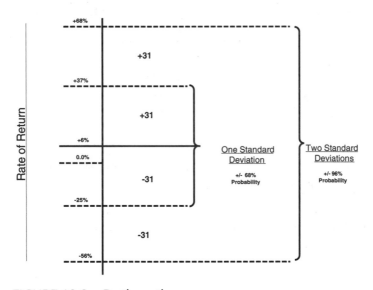

FIGURE 10.2   *Do the math.*

Explain that the average return for Risky Business was 6% (rounded) and its standard deviation is 31. That means that approximately two-thirds of the time, the range of returns for this manager fell within a range of plus-31 and minus-31 from its average return of 6%. That means we have a high of 37% and a low of (25%). To increase our understanding of Risky Business's volatility, let's apply a second standard deviation that takes into account roughly 95% of all probabilities. We add another 31 to the top bringing it to a positive 68%, but we have to subtract 31 from the bottom number, resulting in a negative (56%).

Now you have something to discuss with your client. The client certainly wouldn't be disappointed with the higher end of the returns, but how might they feel about the potential for loss—perhaps more than half the principal value of the portfolio? Without "doing the math" for your client, what on the risk/reward illustration gives them the same level of understanding—the same feeling and sense—for the potential volatility of a manager like Risky Business? I submit, nothing. [And I promise not to start using "I submit."]

After discussing the concept of volatility risk (or standard deviation), continue to expand upon the topic as appropriate by explaining that there are many other facets of risk that you take into consideration as you assist your clients in developing and implementing their wealth management plans.

Those types of risk in addition to volatility, include

interest rate	leverage	management
inflation	cyclical	liquidity
event	regulatory	operational
transparency	currency	style
sociopolitical	concentration	asset allocation methodology
credit	market	

Expert References

Referring to the work or opinion of a noted authority is a credible means of supporting your message; however, some financial professionals are merely name-droppers without explaining the significance of the "name" and the relevance of the person's work.

Consider telling a client, "In 1952, a man by the name of Harry Markowitz developed Modern Portfolio Theory. He received a Nobel Prize for his work creating an efficient frontier of optimal portfolios."

Without further explanation of Markowitz' work, or more importantly, its application to the client's specific situation, this expert reference will have little impact on the client. The client might even be confused at the use of the term "modern." Could something developed in 1952 still be relevant today? While I have nothing but respect for Professor Markowitz and other distinguished financial experts (too numerous to mention), don't trivialize their contributions in an attempt to increase your own credibility.

Financial professionals may reference the outlook and perspective of investment strategists or other noted thought-leaders, especially those within their own firm. There's nothing wrong in this unless your references consist of nothing more than reciting a litany of someone else's predictions and forecasts.

"Our investment strategist thinks the market will end the year at ___; the yield on the 10-Year Treasury will be ___; and GDP will come in at ___."

Clients want to know what you think and want you to support your expert's position with a rationale. Make sure you provide that reasoning and do so by making it your own.

"Our investment strategist thinks the market will end the year at ___ and I agree. Based on current growth rates, inflation expectations, and the expectation of compromise in Washington resulting in sound fiscal and tax policy [wouldn't that be nice?], I want to call your attention to...."

I can't speak for the investment strategists at your firm, but I don't think they'll mind—or at least they shouldn't—if you adopt their work and rationale and present it as your own. If you don't, your clients will always be wondering, "What do you think?" And the strategists, analysts, and thought-leaders at your firm that "get it" encourage you to call them directly and pick their brains, share your thoughts and perspective, and most importantly, let them know how your clients are feeling and behaving so they don't lose sight of what's happening on Main Street.

Reference materials may also support your position and enhance your credibility, but be sure you cite credentials for the material to demonstrate its importance.

For example, suppose you're speaking to a group of fiduciaries and you want to make sure they are aware of their duties and responsibilities and also show them that you understand what they're responsible for. You could use the publication "Prudent Practices for Investment Stewards" written by *fi*360. But how should it be introduced?

"I've passed out a brochure. It's like a fiduciary bible. Now please go to page 10 where your duties and responsibilities are listed."

Or,

"Ladies and gentlemen, I've given each of you an important publication. It's titled 'Prudent Practices for Investment Stewards.' It's for individuals like you who have the legal responsibility for managing someone else's money. The publication was written by *fi*360, an organization dedicated to promoting a culture of fiduciary responsibility and improving the decision making processes of investment fiduciaries. It was technically reviewed by the American Institute of Certified Public Accountants as well as legally substantiated by a major law firm. Please turn to page 10 [then wait until everyone is at page 10—it serves no purpose to keep speaking until everyone is "on the same page with you"]. In the middle of the page you will find seven fiduciary practices, or Global Fiduciary Precepts as they're referred to, that you should be aware of. Let's review each of them."

1. Know standards, laws, and trust provisions.

2. Diversify assets to specific risk/return profile of the client.

3. Prepare an investment policy statement.

4. Use "prudent experts" (for example, an investment manager) and document due diligence.

5. Control and account for expenses.

6. Monitor the activities of "prudent experts."

7. Avoid conflicts of interest and prohibited transactions.

By virtue of their education, training, skill, and experience, referencing individuals and organizations that have expertise and specialized knowledge can be an effective way to support your position. However, remember that your clients are most interested in your opinion as to how the work of these experts applies to their situation.

Statistics, analytics, facts, and expert references are a common and *safe* way to bolster your credibility and strengthen your message. But even when artfully communicated, clients tend to forget these in relatively short order. Another *safe*, but possibly more memorable approach is to develop creative safe harbors and analogies, to tie your message to your clients' feelings, and to share experiences that provide insight into your character and values.

Safe Harbors

The core/universal wealth management value proposition is every financial professional's safe harbor. Another safe harbor—critical if the focus of your practice is in investments and helpful if your focus is in any of the other three cornerstones of wealth—is your ability to render an economic/investment outlook.

What do you see?

I	E	G	
R			

No, it's not an abbreviated Snellen chart used to measure visual acuity. It's a memory reminder that allows you to render a concise and organized overview of the economy and investment markets.

How do you respond when your clients ask you: "What's going on in the market?" Is it possible that their question catches you off guard and your response is vague or too simplistic—perhaps the 20/200 equivalent of the oversized letter at the top of a real eye chart? Or do you delve into the umpteenth degree of detail like the 20/10 line of virtually undecipherable characters? Where do you even start?

Start by thinking of the letter "I" and what it stands for: Interest rates and inflation. Good news, bad, or mixed, clients are always concerned with these two topics. Next, consider what the letter "E" represents: The economy certainly, but that is a broad subject; therefore you can break it into more manageable parts by addressing: Earnings, employment, energy, housing [you get there through "equity extraction," remembering how some people used to think of their home equity as their personal ATM machine], and the election. There's always an election to speak about (at the local, state, or national level) or an election's aftermath and implications on taxes, spending, the debt and deficits, and other topics that affect your clients. Don't forget that while "all politics may be local," we live in a global and interdependent world economy, which brings you to "G." In 2012 that letter sparked continual thoughts of Greece and the crisis within the Euro zone. But through this period, Greece was not the only global story. Think about the Japanese earthquake and tsunami, or the Arab Spring; increasing tension with Iran; the killing of bin Laden; and the war on terrorism, oh and granted back to Greece [enough of Greece already]. That's the beauty of I, E, and G. It prompts you to think and speak about those matters that are on the minds of your clients, but instead of the often sensationalized way those topics are portrayed in the media, let yours be the voice of calm, concise, and considered reason. That brings you to the most important element of your statement represented by the oversized letter "R," which stands for risk.

Remind your clients that there have always been risks in the markets. There always will be, and there sure seems to be more than our fair share of it in the economy and markets today. Remind your clients that people have always had excuses not to invest or carry out their plans because of risks—real or perceived—associated with conflicts and crises; bubbles and binges; and disasters (natural and manmade). Remind your clients how you carefully observe, study, and examine ways to deal with risk, and that the best way to do so is to adhere to your process—a process that begins by listening and understanding your clients and their concerns and then analyzing their situation and developing solutions to help them achieve their goals and objectives. With their agreement you execute those solutions in an independent, objective, and unbiased manner always mindful of controlling costs and expenses. And you continually monitor the progress of your clients' plans making appropriate adjustments in response to material market conditions, changes in tax laws or regulations, and changes that will inevitably occur in the lives of your clients and their family members. You do all that, because it's the best way to deal with risk.

I was visiting recently with a fine team of financial professionals who use the *IEGR method*. They prepare a one-page summary and tape it on top of the pull-out leafs in their desks for quick reference anytime a client calls with concerns about the markets. They prepare a new summary each week as they read through all the literature, articles, journals, and other sources of information they rely on. It has become their guide to "separating the wheat from the chaff," focusing on the most useful and valuable information rather than getting bogged down with mind-numbing prognostications, forecasts, estimates, and best guesses. They admit, however, that they seldom refer to the summary because the simple process they go through in preparing it ingrains it in their memories, making their recall a snap.

Other Safe Harbor Subjects

You know better than anyone the topics that you frequently discuss with your clients. The following list is partial.

Investments	Banking, credit, lending, and liability management
Asset allocation/ diversification	Cash management
Active/passive investing	Mortgages, lines of credit
Investment styles	Business financing
Risk management	**Trust, estate, and fiduciary services**
Life insurance	Estate and gift planning
Disability insurance	Elder care
Asset and income protection strategies	Charitable giving

Compile your list of recurring topics and craft streamlined explanations for each, stressing no more than three or four key points that can be delivered in 10 minutes or less. That is going to require you to cut out any superfluous information. Time that's wasted on meaningless generalities or excessive detail is time that detracts from and obscures the message that you need to convey. Your well-constructed *safe harbor* presentations can always be expanded upon when necessary, but financial professionals may have trouble discerning what is necessary from what is too little or too much information. When in doubt, focus on high-level, key points—the essence of what matters most to the client.

Analogies

I have heard some fine analogies and, unfortunately, all too many of the worst that financial professionals use to help support their message. Analogies create visual imagery within your clients' minds and foster better understanding of what you're explaining by referencing the familiar to help your clients better understand a point.

Many financial professionals still use trite analogies, such as "don't put all your eggs in one basket," because it takes very little thought, and clients are so familiar with it. But there's another idiom that applies that negates the intended effect: "Familiarity breeds contempt," that is, that concept is so overused that clients don't appreciate it. They may also be disappointed in your reliance on such a simple illustration of the dangers of a concentrated portfolio. You should always remember what Einstein said about making things easy to understand, but some analogies are too simplistic and you risk diminishing your stature and credibility by using them.

How about this one:

"Let's assume that you're the manager of a baseball team and you fill out your lineup with a pitcher, catcher, and seven right fielders. While they all might be good right fielders, you would never field a team like that. When it comes to your investments, would you only want to own 7 of the same types of stocks and virtually nothing else?"

This isn't fictitious. I overheard one top financial professional saying this to a client (and I've heard many iterations of the analogy delivered by other financial professionals).

The analogy is a poor one because your clients know you wouldn't field a team with seven of the same position players. It is a case of "dumbing down" an already trite analogy. Your clients expect and deserve better from you. Faced with having to advise a client about the risks associated with a concentrated portfolio, opting for a facts-driven argument instead of using a weak analogy would be a better approach. It would be easy to remind the client of the dangers of concentrated positions by making specific reference to the corporate graveyards filled with the noted and the notorious (e.g., Enron, WorldCom, Adelphia, Madoff Investment Securities, Stanford Financial Group, and unfortunately, dozens more).

Suppose you're pursuing a relationship with a new client who tells you they're firing their investment advisor due to the underperformance, expense, and time required to monitor their actively managed investment portfolio consisting of separately managed accounts and mutual funds. Through your discovery process, you've determined that the client feels very strongly about his position, although you have always been a strong advocate for professionally managed investment portfolios. What do you do? Give the client what he wants, try to convince him that he's wrong, or give the client something else to consider?

Consider first acknowledging the merit in the client's position. This demonstrates not only that you're a good listener, but also that you respect the client's position. But then you could tell him

"I was reading an article about our war on terrorism and the military's use of drone aircraft. The article addressed the increased usage of these unmanned aircraft and reported positive mission performance rates, reduction in costs, and the ability to conduct missions without putting pilots in the cockpit and in harm's way. But next to a picture of a drone, there was also a picture of a twin-engine Beechcraft propeller plane that the military had recently purchased, retrofitted, and put into operation. The article explained that these aircraft were being deployed on missions with pilots in the cockpit at the controls, because the military determined that in some situations, actively managed aircraft can respond in ways that even the most technically advanced drone cannot. The military determined that having both the unmanned drones and the manned aircraft in its arsenal gives it better operational capability than having just one or the other. I think it makes sense to consider the same rationale when constructing portfolios for my clients. Clearly, as you have pointed out, there are many advantages to using passively managed investment vehicles, but we should recognize that actively managed investments may have a place in your portfolio as well. Now you could very well have the wrong money managers or funds—I just don't know at this juncture—but I'll do a thorough examination of your managers and give you my opinion in that regard. At this point, however, I think we should keep all of our options—active, passive, or a combination of the two—on the table so that we have the best operational capability as we reconstruct your investment portfolio."

I spoke to another financial professional about analogies and he asked for my opinion about one he used during a conversation with one of his clients who came to see him about her imminent retirement:

"You must be looking forward to moving to your new home at the Shore. What type of water sports do you enjoy?" he asked.

He found her response somewhat surprising: "I barely go near the water. I like to walk along the beach, but I'm about as afraid of the water as I am of investing in the market. That's why I'd prefer to keep my investments as safe and conservative as possible."

"I understand how you feel," he told her as he drew on a legal pad a sketch representing the beach and the ocean. "You feel safe and comfortable walking along the beach, and in implementing a long-term investment plan for your retirement, we'll consider those types of investments that will give you that same strong sense of safety and security. But let me ask you, when you're walking on the beach do you ever wade into the surf— not far, maybe up to your ankles or so? Sure, you still feel very safe doing that."

Drawing a line from the "shoreline" out just an inch or so into the "water," he continued: "As we've discussed your long-term spending needs, it may be necessary to invest in some high-quality, dividend paying stocks and high-quality bonds, for example, in an effort to generate the type of income that my analysis of your situation indicates you'll need to maintain the standard of living you want throughout your retirement. Think of those types of investments as being in close to the Shore, like where you walk in the surf."

Then drawing another line, an inch further out in the water, he continued: "While I sense you'd be comfortable with your investments on the beach and just a little way out in the water, I have to ask you if you would consider moving out a little farther into the water—let's say up to your knees? I know that you would prefer not to do so if you don't have to, but you may have to move out a little farther in the investment waters because the analyses I've run for your retirement suggest you might not be able to do everything you want including helping your children and grandchildren and supporting important charitable causes you've told me about. To have a greater likelihood of being able to realize those objectives, we may have to add investments to protect the purchasing power of your assets as well as provide an opportunity for conservative growth. But past this point, you would never go into the deeper waters, and from an investment perspective I will do everything I can to see that you never get in over your head."

I liked the analogy, and I asked him what happened with the client. He told me she's enjoying her retirement and that they talk frequently. From time to time she'll ask him about some investment she was reading about or a "tip" she got from a friend wanting to know where it would fit: On her beach, in the shallow waters, or would it be in the deep water far too risky for her to consider? This is an example of a relationship-enduring analogy that struck a chord with the client that continues to resonate.

Feelings

Prospective clients come to you wounded, and your current clients were once prospective. Their financial trauma may have been self-inflicted or administered by third parties. Their wounds may stem from erratic behavior, poor behavior, or poor advice. They may be victims of overconfidence, wishful thinking, a difficult environment, or just plain old bad luck. They may wear their feelings on their sleeves and keep others repressed, but they are always there.

Yet when financial professionals render their advice, so much of the appeal is based on logic and reasoning. You focus brilliantly on the data, studies, simulations, and expert references to validate your recommendations, but if you fail to address your clients' feelings you don't serve the whole client. You need to address not only the objective elements of a case, but also acknowledge, respect, and solve the emotional elements.

Personal Experiences and the "Fifth Element"

There's one more way to play it *safe*, but its use should be saved for exceptional occasions. While you always endeavor to understand and empathize with your clients, there may be times when you have personally experienced something in your life or practice that has left its imprint on your character, your values, and your beliefs. And sometimes, when you're listening to your clients, a nerve is touched or a memory rekindled, and you identify with them in a special and personal way.

I'm not describing the "Oh, that happened to me too," reflex to common occurrences that serve little purpose except to divert attention from where it belongs to you. I'm referring to something much deeper, something that defines your character, reveals your sensitivity, and demonstrates an acute awareness to which only you and this specific client can relate.

It enables you to respond to your client because you have walked in their shoes. You or someone dear to you has confronted their challenges and faced their fears and shed the same tears. And you made it through, perhaps by yourself or perhaps with the help of someone who you could not have done it without and it changed you. It transformed you and all you stand for and believe in.

No one can give you that experience or this "fifth element" to your value proposition, and you may not have one, at least not yet. But if you do and only if the circumstances are befitting, sharing this with your client can form a bridge of understanding, respect, and trust that will span your relationship.

Endnote

1. Attributed in S. F. Witseson, D. L. Kigar, and T. Harvey, "The Exceptional Brain of Albert Einstein," *British Medical Journal*, October 1999.

Chapter 11

It's Showtime!

All the world's a stage...
—William Shakespeare, *As You Like It*

I t's showtime!

Whether you're presenting to an individual or a couple in the sanctum of your office; to a small group cloistered in a conference room; or an assembly gathered around you to consider your thoughts, you're on stage, you're acting, and you're playing the title role.

There is nothing wrong with acting. Anything less than delivering your best performance is a disservice to your clients who pay good money to be with you. Disappoint them once, twice, too many times, and you place your relationship in jeopardy. Think your personal performance doesn't matter? Then don't be surprised when your audience stops showing up.

"My clients want me—the real me—not some phony, artificial version," is what I hear from financial

159

professionals taken aback by the notion that they should act otherwise. I emphatically agree, but are you being insincere or phony when you tell your clients how much you care about them? Of course you care about them, and now you understand that critical listening is one way to prove it. Critical listening skills aren't phony or artificial; they're artful, professional, and respect-ful—and they won't go unnoticed. The same is true of the use of critical speaking skills, and when they are combined with thoughtful and creative presentation tactics you provide your clients with the best seat in the house for the most important play in town—a play that's all about them.

Winning and Losing Presentation Tactics

Critical Openers

In one-on-one, one-on-two, and small group presenta-tions, consider using a Critical Opener with

- Prospective clients

- Existing clients

- Small, select audiences

- Management, colleagues, and team members

Prospective Clients

Prospective clients aren't meeting with you to tell you how good they feel about their financial affairs, yet they may be hesitant to bring up their issues and concerns for fear of looking bad. In the discovery phase of your relationship, encouraging them to tell you about their problems and disappointments serves not only to provide you with critical information and insight into their feelings, it enables clients to vent, to listen to themselves, and to realize that they shouldn't be satisfied with the way things are and that it's time to change

In subsequent meetings with prospective clients, modify your Critical Opener by prefacing your declaration of readiness, with a summary of the most pertinent facts and feelings your clients shared with you—the attuned feedback—in previous conversations.

"When we were last together, you shared with me your concerns about your current situation [and then reiterate their concerns]."

Then let them know, "I've been doing a lot of thinking about what you said and analyzing the information you gave me. I've been exploring ways to help you resolve these issues and implement an appropriate plan of action to help you achieve your goals and objectives, and I'm fully prepared to discuss my findings and suggestions with you this morning."

Finishing your Critical Opener—"Before we get into any of that, please tell me, what else is on your mind that we should discuss today? Because I want to be sure that we're focusing on those matters that are most important to you."

Notice in this example, the invitation to share any new thoughts or issues precedes the statement of benefit, that is, "to always focus on those matters that are most important" to the client.

Existing Clients

Even though you go to great lengths to prepare for your periodic reviews with existing clients, over time these reviews can become mechanical and routine. And with online account access, clients know how their accounts are performing well before they walk into your office. So you could be focusing on what may be old news to them. Using a Critical Opener reminds your clients that their agenda always supersedes the one you prepared for them, but more importantly, it may lead to discussions about matters that may never have surfaced simply because you never asked.

"I'm fully prepared to discuss the quarterly performance of all of your accounts and to review our progress in meeting your goals and objectives."

At that point recap key points from previous meetings or conversations to jog their memory and set the stage for today's discussions.

"You'll recall that during our previous meeting we discussed…and we decided to continue to…. Before we get into the review, please tell me is there anything else we should discuss today? I want to make sure that we cover everything that's important to you."

Notice that in the above example, the simple request was phrased in the form of a close-ended question since your clients could respond, "No." Is that a big problem? Probably not, but you can easily make it an open-ended inquiry by saying "what else would you like to talk about today?"

The worst that can happen in either case is that your clients tell you they don't have anything else they want to discuss, which now gives you permission to proceed with your review or presentation. But if they do raise new issues or ideas, you know them up front, and, true to your word, you address those matters that are impor-tant to them.

Small, Select Audiences

Many financial professionals serve on boards and committees for various civic, social, charitable, and religious entities. While the dynamics of collective decision-making are beyond the scope of this book, when you have the opportunity to present your position or lead a discussion on a particular subject, begin with a Critical Opener to engage your fellow board or committee members instead of lecturing them.

"The Chair has asked me to lead a discussion this evening on the opportunities and challenges we face with the upcoming fundraising campaign. I've prepared an agenda and am fully prepared to discuss each item; however, I'd like to know how each of you feels about the campaign. Your thoughts and perspectives are just as important as any of mine. Mary, please be so kind as to start us off by sharing your thoughts about the campaign with us?"

Management, Colleagues, and Team Members

Critical Openers come in handy when you're meeting with a manager, your colleagues, or team members to discuss, for example, a new business development opportunity.

"I'm fully prepared to discuss the proposal I've developed for the Big New Opportunity. I want to make sure that we address those aspects of the case that you deem critical to our success. Please share your thoughts and ideas with me so that we can address those points most important to you."

I used this approach with a new manager who asked for a full review of all the capabilities and services of my group. I created a detailed PowerPoint presentation along with collateral materials to present to him, but then I wondered, what did he want to get out of the meeting—a big information dump or something more specific? Why not just ask?

"As you requested, I've come fully prepared to discuss the comprehensive services and capabilities that my team offers our clients. However, to make sure that the time you've set aside this afternoon is used most wisely, please tell me how you see the team helping you drive the company's main client service objectives? By doing so, we'll focus on those matters that are most important to you."

45 minutes later, my manager stopped talking. And during those 45 minutes, I learned about the items that were most important to him. Fortunately, I had prepared for those matters, and that's where I focused the remainder of our time. Was I disappointed I didn't get a chance to go through my slides and all the other material that I prepared? Not at all. And my manager didn't question the rest of my plans for the team because professionals respect fellow professionals, and he knew that I had done the work and could support it with all the details if he ever needed me to.

Larger Audiences

In larger group settings opening with a Critical Opener is often impractical because of the size of your audience. Do you want to trust the few people who might speak up to represent the group at-large? Or will anyone speak up leaving you in awkward silence? One pseudo-version of a Critical Opener is when a speaker begins by saying that instead of delivering any prepared remarks, he would just like to take questions from the audience and make it a more informal discussion. In my opinion, that's a sign that he came unprepared and would prefer to take his chances winging it in Q&A.

Social Politeness, Pleasantries, and Banter

Social politeness, pleasantries, and banter are ice-breaking and rapport-building norms that vary with each interaction with a client or group. They should take place as you deem fit, but they should never replace your opening statement.

Opening Statements

At some point your clients are expecting you to "blow the whistle," end the casual non-business conversation, and begin your presentation, and this is not how you want to begin:

"My name is Bob Rednif and I'm with Financial Services, Ltd., and it's a real pleasure for me to be with you today. Thanks for inviting me to meet with you. I thought what I'd do today is talk a little bit about my firm, our philosophy and service model, and how we help clients just like you. How does that sound?"

It sounds trite and conventional, but financial professionals open like that all the time. In an effort to not sound too formal, you gravitate to the other extreme and sound too informal especially when you're dealing with a subject as important as your clients' wealth. Think about it—as you always should—from your clients' perspective. What do they expect—a degree of formality from you when you're speaking about their million or five million or ten million dollar portfolios, or casual nonchalance?

This type of opening is like a "false green" in golf. You think you've landed your ball on the green and are in good position to score, only your ball begins rolling back and suddenly it's off the green way down the fairway (or into the rough or hazard), leaving you with a troublesome and awkward next shot. The trouble with *false openings* is that when you're finished, you have to open for real, and you're often unprepared to do so.

Seldom is there a good recovery from a false opening. Instead what typically happens is you get right into your prepared materials—handouts, pitch books, or slides—and go through them page by page, slide by slide.

There's nothing wrong with doing that provided you want to look and sound just like all the other financial professionals who have come before or will follow you—all except for a pair of presenters who earned the dubious distinction of making it onto the financial professionals' "Wall of Presentation Shame" for their following statement and actions:

> "We prepared some materials for you and why don't you go ahead and feel free to flip through them as we talk."
>
> And flip he did, and talk they did. If only you could have seen the expression of bewilderment on the prospect's [never to become a client's] face throughout their presentation.

The ignominious tandem took comfort in the conventionality of their standard presentation materials, but their unconventional approach is not quite what John Maynard Keynes had in mind.

> *Worldly wisdom teaches that it is better for the reputation to fail conventionally than to succeed unconventionally.*
> —John Maynard Keynes, *The General Theory of Employment, Interest, and Money,* 1936

Your opening statement sets the tenor for your entire presentation. It signals your insight and creativity, your concern and understanding, and your conviction and confidence that together you and your clients (or you and your audience) can accomplish great things.

And while your process of developing and implementing the course of action you propose is grounded in the core tenets of your practice, what makes your approach unconventional is how you identify and address unique and distinct touchpoints that resonate with your clients or audience.

Be Creative

It was 4:30 in the afternoon; the family had been sequestered in their attorney's conference room for the better part of the entire day listening to "the finalists" make their presentations, explaining why each should be the chosen one.

Ours was the last of the presentations. Some say we had an advantage because clients are more apt to remember the last presentation, but if you had seen the weary and tired gazes that greeted us, you would wonder, like we did, if they would be able (or want) to stay awake through another presentation.

All the presenters were expected to bring a PowerPoint presentation and we did, but we had the good fortune of not being able to get the presentation to transfer to the computer (or from the computer to the projector) so we just shut it down and went without. We passed out the obligatory presentation books along with a key chain to each member of the family and their attorney. The key chain had a small Rubik's cube as the pendant, and we had a regular-sized cube that we referred to as we described the twists and turns of the family's financial situation: fortunes made and lost, then made again; the family dynamics—first and second marriages, children, step-children, grandchildren (of his, hers, and theirs), and siblings (and business partners); multiple investment accounts and trust funds with specific objectives, guidelines, and beneficiaries; and a host of other wealth management issues relating to the family's real estate and business interest. With each reference we twisted or turned the cube.

I won't describe the courses of action we proposed because that would take a small book in itself, but to fast-forward to our closing statement, when my colleague picked up the cube he positioned it behind his back and then recapped all of the family's challenges, the solutions that we proposed, and the process by which we would implement and monitor progress. With each major point, everyone could tell he was turning a portion of the cube...until? He unveiled a still unsolved Cube apologizing for not being a better puzzle-solver, but promising the family that he and his team would work tirelessly on their behalf to solve the complex financial puzzles confronting them.

Did we win that relationship? Yes. Was it because of the Rubik's cube? Maybe, maybe not. There's no doubt all the firms competing for the relationship were well-qualified and up to the task. But I think that we were remembered. Perhaps that evening or the next day as the family members were contemplating which firm to choose, they picked up their key chain and began to play with the cube and thought about us.

By the way, the senior partner of our team was not as pleased with our presentation as we were until he heard the good news days later. He expected us to solve the cube as the climax to our presentation. I guess that's why he's the senior partner.

Be Organized

Remember the KISS principle? Nowhere is it more applicable than in structuring the framework of a presentation.

- Critical Opening/Opening Statement
- Address Critical Point 1/Solve
- Address Critical Point 2/Solve
- Address Critical Point 3/Solve; and if necessary
- Address Critical Point 4/Solve
- Questions
- Closing Statement

But KISS is diametrically at odds with a financial professional's desire to solve as many of the clients' financial needs and problems as possible, and when you give into the temptation your presentation can resemble a smorgasbord. Have you eaten at a smorgasbord recently? Why not? Seems like a good idea—lots and lots of food. But then you get in line, and it's one dish after another—so much to consider, so much to choose from. But how will it all taste together? Can you even tell what you're eating after a while? How do you feel afterwards? Are you satisfied or just stuffed? Are you happy and content or would you rather not say? Don't leave your clients feeling like they've just experienced a verbal smorgasbord that they can't digest.

That's one of the problems with presentations delivered by team members from different disciplines. Each presentation has merit, but does each bear equal importance to the client at the time? If they don't, leave the less timely or less important parts out. Win the relationship and address those other matters at another time when they will be the primary focus of your presentation.

Giving a client too much to consume, too much to think about is a recipe for indecision and possibly rejection.

I have to bestow another financial professional "Wall of Presentation Shame" award on a team who just about threw everything except the kitchen sink at their prospective clients.

> After a dizzying assault of one issue and its multi-faceted solution after another presented in rapid-fire succession aided by a full battery of indecipherable PowerPoint charts, the lead financial professional interrupted one of her colleagues and said: "You guys' [nice English] eyes look glazed over. Would you like us to stop?" And the response was "Yes," and I'm convinced the client was serious, but she simply chuckled and the presentation continued for another 30 minutes.

That presentation had just about everything going wrong for it. No one took responsibility for ensuring an orderly flow of critical subject matter. Instead, everyone was allowed to speak and contribute something even if they were poor speakers and had little to say. Moreover, no one had the courage to step in during the presentation and call an audible to get it back on track. The number of PowerPoint slides would have been borderline comical, if it wasn't for the fact that you couldn't read the slides. So several presenters took care of that by turning their back to the clients and reading the entire text of the slides verbatim. I agree with Christopher

Witt who wrote *Real Leaders Don't Do PowerPoint* (Crown Business, 2009). PowerPoint is just a tool, an option that good speakers can use if necessary, but it never compensates for nor excuses poor presentation skills.

And finally this presentation just went on and on in spite of the client's exhortations to stop.

Be Concise

Financial professionals would be revered as heroes if they kept their presentations down to 18 minutes, which Granville N. Toogood wrote about in his book *The New Articulate Executive* (McGraw-Hill, 2010). According to a study by the U.S. Navy, "in a classroom, presentation or lecture environment, an audience's ability to focus on what the speaker is saying and then remember what was said drops off at eighteen minutes like the continental shelf plunging straight down into the abyss."

Think about the last time you were on the receiving end of a presentation or a speech. How long was it before you were checking your watch, checking your smartphone, or simply checking out? How often have you wished a speaker would go longer than the allocated time? Are you ever disappointed when a speaker finishes early (or do they ever)? Does the speaker's energy level increase or decrease over time, and what about your energy level as a listener?

Is the problem that you have too much that needs to be said and that it takes far more than 18 minutes to say it? Or would that be plenty of time if you didn't waste so much of it?

Woodrow Wilson said, "If I am to speak 10 minutes, I need a week for preparation. If 15 minutes, three days. If half an hour, two days. If an hour, I'm ready now."

How could the President get away speaking for an hour without preparing?

Filler, plenty of filler.

All too often "filler" infiltrates your presentations and speech. Filler absorbs your clients' attention and leaves them oblivious to your intended message.

But "I don't have days to prepare for my presentation."

I understand, but you don't always need days to do so. Remember why you develop *safe harbor* presentations—crisp, clear, concise explanations of critical recurring subject matter. Draw upon your safe harbors, and all you have to do is add the facts and feelings of your clients' situation to make compelling and relevant presentations.

Be aware of the clock and monitor your time and energy level (see Figure 11.1).

Begin your presentation in the engagement zone with a strong and provocative opening instead of a common or weak *false opening*.

Use your critical speaking skills to maintain your energy level—especially eye engagement, gestures, volume, inflection, and pace. But recognize that it's easy to drift into the danger zone especially when you're using statistics and analytics to support your position.

Because of that, there's a tendency to hurry through your explanation—don't. Take your time. Remember what Einstein said, and be the first financial professional to make the technical clear and easy for your clients to understand.

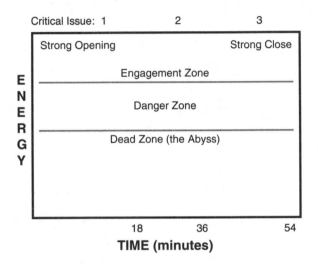

FIGURE 11.1   *Presentation zones.*

As you come to the end of your remarks on the first critical issue, realize that your energy levels tend to drop when an end—intermediate or final—is in sight. Don't succumb. Make sure that your energy rises into the engagement zone as you begin making your case on the next critical issue. In that way, longer presentations become a series of two, three (or four) strong mini-presentations all connected by a major theme or purpose.

And Be Prepared to Close

The end of your presentation is just moments away. You've done it—well almost. Now be prepared to close, but never close on Q&A.

"Thank you very much for your attention, I'm delighted to take any questions you may have."

And then what happens if you don't get any questions, or if you get a trivial question or an argumentative question? Is that how you want to finish? Is that the last impression you want your clients or audience to remember of you?

Here's what you say.

"Before I leave you with my final thoughts on my recommendation and the course of action I've laid out for you, I welcome your thoughts, comments, or questions."

Notice how you politely let your clients or audience know that you will have the final word. And notice also that you invite not only questions, but their thoughts or comments because you want them to know you anticipate positive remarks and feedback, not just questions.

Then after the last question, it's time to close. Pause, engage the sclera, and deliver your call to action with the same eloquence and passion that you opened your presentation with, and by all means, know your close cold—never read or be note dependent. It never ceases to amaze me that financial professionals think their opening and their close will just "come to them." It doesn't happen. Developing and mastering your opening and closing statement takes time, patience, imagination, and practice.

A final point about your close: Once you've delivered it, your presentation is over. Don't say or add anything else. It won't add to your presentation; it will only detract and leave your clients or audience wondering if there's anything else you left out.

Chapter 12

Wise Emperors

How do you get to Carnegie Hall?
Practice, Practice, Practice.

To say I've thrown a lot at you and that I expect a lot from you is an understatement. I also know how much your clients throw at you, and they expect even more. But only you know if you've got what it takes to take your communication skills to the next level. I suspect you do, but it won't be easy.

As I was finishing this book, the Wimbledon Men's Singles Championship had just been played between Roger Federer, arguably the greatest tennis player of all time, and Andy Murray, a perennial Top 4 in the World, three time major championship finalist, and Britain's greatest hope to end a 76-year draught of a native born champion.

Federer won the match and a record-tying seventh Wimbledon championship, and I should probably find something in Federer's technique and methods to extrapolate and share with you to improve your communication (if not your racquet) skills. But I've chosen to do so with Murray instead, because my eye caught an article written by Tom Perotta in *The Wall Street Journal* titled "Cracking Tennis's Inner Circle," back on March 23, 2012. The article describes Murray's relationship with his new coach, Ivan Lendl, a Hall-of-Famer tennis player who wants Murray to focus on three things:

1. His forehand;

2. Finishing long matches; and

3. Exhibiting less negative energy.

I found each of those points interesting and informative not just for Murray, but for financial professionals who want to improve their communication skills.

Yet I wondered, why would a world-class player like Murray need to work on the most fundamental shot in the game—a shot he's hit millions of times? Exactly because it is so fundamental sometimes even the pros take it for granted. Mastering your *safe harbor* subject matter is like your forehand; it's fundamental to your game as it has to be there when you need it.

Murray is also notorious for futzing around on the court, taking too long to finish his matches, giving lesser opponents a chance to upset him and draining him of his physical reserves and energy. Lendl wants him to stay focused and reduce careless and costly lapses of attention, just as you have to stay focused and avoid lapses of attention when you're listening to your clients. You can't be thinking about what you're going to say next or what question you should ask when they finish talking; you can't let your mind wander—not on anything. You never know when a crucial point in a conversation or a tennis match will occur; that's why you have to be focused and in the game at all times.

All tennis players when they see their opponents' heads drop, their shoulders sag—that worrie me look that says they just want to get off the court—become inspired and grow more confident. Unfortunately negative energy conveyed by your facial and vocal expressions conveys just the opposite in your clients.

Murray may not have won Wimbledon or a major championship—yet, but you have to like his chances and admire his determination for pushing himself and not settling for less.[1]

"Do You Really Want to Know?"

If you ask a colleague or a team member if you're a good speaker (or even a good listener), chances are high that they'll say you are. Behind your back they may say something different, but to your face, looking you right in the eye, they'll offer kind words of praise and encouragement. Just what you wanted and expected. And don't you find yourself doing the same when the tables are turned? Why? Because critiquing someone is hard. It's hard because "constructive criticism" is an oxymoron: "constructive" is positive; "criticism" is negative. It's difficult to give because you don't want to hurt someone's feelings and have them take it personally, so you try to accentuate the positive and disregard the negative. You think you're doing your colleagues and team members a favor, as they think they're doing you one.

Your success is an impediment to asking for, receiving, and accepting constructive criticism. Why tamper with success, and who is courageous enough to "tell the Emperor he has no clothes" or at least that his royal garb is wrinkled and he's talking over his subjects' heads? You're the Emperor and you're doing a lot of things right. But wise Emperors never take for granted their loyal subjects or their loyal clients; wise Emperors always seek sound advice and counsel.

Instead of asking for someone's feedback, try explaining what you're concerned about or what you want to improve upon: "I know that I speak too fast. I always have. If you were a client or prospective client, how would you feel about that? What would you like to tell me?"

They now have your express permission to respond objectively and, if appropriate, to respond critically for constructive purposes:

"Since you asked, from a client's perspective you do speak very fast. Even I have a hard time keeping up with you, and I have a pretty good idea what you're talking about—much better than I assume your clients do. And frankly, listening to you for too long is exhausting. I recognize that you're smart, but we're all just mere mortals. Slow down and let your points sink in."

Or how about—

"I was reading somewhere that finishing your sentences with 'okays' and 'all rights' can be distracting to the listener. Am I in that camp and does that distract you?"

Suppose you did find it distracting, but instead of being asked for your opinion as above, you came right out and volunteered it: "I was listening to your presentation today and while you covered some very interesting points, all those 'okays' and 'all rights' were very distracting. I counted 37 of them in a 10-minute time span alone."

Unsolicited the speaker might respond, "Screw you, who asked for your two cents?" But you'll respond differently when you do ask for a colleague's opinion.

Candid Camera

Candid Camera was a hidden camera/practical joke reality TV series that first aired in 1948, but began on radio as *Candid Microphone* a year earlier. While the show laughed at people doing and saying things in awkward situations, there's nothing funny about exhibiting poor communication skills in real life in front of clients. While I'm not suggesting that you video-record actual client meetings, I strongly recommend you tape your presentations beforehand for practice and review.

Professionals in all walks of life study and analyze film to identify flaws and deficiencies in their performances. Why should financial professionals be the exception?

I often hear financial professionals claim that taping presentations and role-plays for practice is fake and artificial and doesn't fairly portray the quality of their work. But how would you feel if the Captain and First

Officer on your next flight weren't required to recertify on a flight simulator twice a year?

Several years ago, after listening to a lecture on presentation skills, I asked the presenter if he'd be kind enough to tape and critique one of my standard presentations. He graciously agreed, and when the day of my appointment arrived I confidently strode into his office and the conference room where his video camera was set up—just he and I and the camera, what could be easier than that? The first "take" didn't last very long, you see I stumbled a bit with the opening—I thought it would just come to me—and asked if we could start again. The second take also didn't get very far, because I repeated what I'd already said, and I asked if I could have another do-over. The third and the fourth and the fifth takes all ended about the same just as I thought my career was about to. Then I thought to myself, of course I got a little nervous, I'd never done this before. I'm sure I'm better in real life. But I knew that I wasn't better in real life—that what I saw and heard was close to what my clients were seeing and hearing, and I wasn't pleased. They deserved better.

Not long after, I gave a presentation to a large group of colleagues gathered from throughout the country in our home office. I wrote out my entire speech, edited and revised it dozens of times until I had just what I wanted, and then I taped myself delivering it—actually, I taped myself reading it. I was pleased with what I saw and heard. I was so familiar with the script, I was able to make a lot of eye contact. My pace and inflection flowed nicely with the message. I was ready to go. Then one of my colleagues whom I showed the tape to asked me, "What if there's no podium in the room?" And terror coursed through my veins as I realized I was 100% note dependent and just, what if, there wasn't a podium to hide behind?

Another interesting experiment to do with a tape of yourself is to watch it without the audio. Just look at yourself. See yourself as your clients do. Would you say there is a *presence* about you, that you look comfortable and confident in your own skin? Then turn off the video and just listen. If it must, can your speech alone carry your message—connect with, move, and inspire your clients? Or do elements of your speaking style make your message difficult or distracting to follow?

Endnote

1. Only a few weeks later, as I was in the editing process, the world watched Murray stand on the gold medal stand, having defeated Federer at the London Olympics.

Let the Dance Begin

Life is the dancer and you are the dance.
—Eckhart Tolle, *A New Earth: Awakening Your Life's Purpose*, 2005

"The Beginning"

You're competitive, driven, and hard-working. You care about your clients and are focused on doing what's right for them. You invest heavily both your time and resources in professional development and practice management. But what else can you do?

Other firms may be bigger and have greater capabilities, stronger reputations and standing in your community, even a more recognizable brand than yours. Or they may be smaller, more agile and responsive to the needs of their financial professionals and the clients they serve. That's how it may be or that's how it may appear looking from the outside in. But what if you're already there or you find the ideal firm in which to practice? What else can you do?

It's a new beginning and with it you have made a steadfast commitment to four critical imperatives:

> You will be clear about who you are and what you do.
>
> You will prove that you are listening to your clients.
>
> You will speak with more confidence, poise, and clarity.
>
> You will always practice.

You help your clients build, manage, protect, and transition wealth. You may be a generalist or you may specialize or concentrate in one of the disciplines of wealth management, but you're always thinking about how you and your colleagues can serve these fundamental needs.

You never refer to yourself as just a "broker," or a money manager, banker, insurance specialist, or trust officer. You're a wealth manager specializing in investments, private banking services, risk management, or trust, estate, and fiduciary services.

You enhance your ability to serve your clients through unfettered listening. You don't filter what you hear, you feel it. You don't challenge what you hear, you accept it. You don't comment on what you hear except to acknowledge its importance to your clients and to you. Your listening skills improve your problem-solving skills as you serve more of your clients' wealth management needs.

When you deliver advice, you deliver it simply. When you state your case, you state it firmly. When you support your position, you present your evidence clearly. And when you speak, your eyes tell all.

You will never stop practicing. Why? Because listening and speaking are skills requiring constant attention; because your field of knowledge is constantly expanding; and because the only constant in your clients' lives is change.

When you practice you sweat, and perhaps, contrary to popular opinion, you will sweat the small stuff because you know that little things matter. Your clients want to like, trust, and respect you, and they used to give you the benefit of any doubt—but no longer. They've become more demanding, more discerning, and more diligent in choosing their financial professionals, and they're keeping score.

That thought takes me back to my days as a championship figure skater—not really, I can't even stand up on a pair of skates, but I do like watching figure skating. I know that in the past, each skater began his or her performance with a perfect score, and the judges took deductions based on technical merit, composition, and style.

Among the many facets of a performance that the judges watched for were

- Clean take-offs and landings (similar to your opening and closing statements)

- The difficulty of a jump or maneuver (akin to your challenge of taking complex, technical subjects and making them easy for your clients)

- Quickness, foot speed; change of direction; the number and positions of movements (which equate to the mannerisms of your speech such as your pace, inflection and volume; and the mannerisms of your body language such as your gestures, stance and posture)

- Creativity and flow of the performance and whether it was delivered with confidence, carriage and style (which is what you want your clients to say about your performance)

I had always been grateful that my clients weren't keeping score of my presentations. Then I realized, of course, they are. They may not have paper or electronic scorecards in front of them, but they're keeping score mentally. And while it may seem insignificant to be dinged here (for lack of eye contact or insistent use of non-words) or nicked there (for playing it too safe or not giving it your all), in the end it all adds up. But unlike figure skating judges, your clients don't award you a silver or bronze medal. They want the gold medal financial professional. With competition that tight it pays to sweat the small stuff.

Now that you've finished the book, it's worth revisiting what I said in the Introduction. Rethink the following with your fresh perspective.

You will never again communicate nor define yourself as you once did. Your clients see and listen to you as never before. Your counsel has never been clearer or more clearly understood. You are more attuned to your clients and your ability to serve them. You exude passion and conviction, your emotions are contagious, your professionalism unmatched. Go ahead, pinch yourself—it's true—you've finally learned to dance.

Throughout your career you've been following directions, taking one step then another, doing what you were taught, what you learned, and what you do the best, but something was missing until now—your *identity*. You befriended your clients, but never as best friends. You filled the part, but never played the role. You spoke of facts, but your words lacked feelings. You sought self-control, but faltered in self-absorption.

The movement of your body is now in rhythm with your speech. Your facial expressions receive and emit emotion. You express and share ideas with ease. You relish the interaction. Practice and performance have merged into one. You communicate with your clients at a highly evolved state.

You hear your clients as you would wish to be heard. You understand their fears and concerns; their dreams and hopes are yours. You're committed to learning about your clients without prying or intruding. You inquire simply, devoting your attention to their answers not the formulation of your questions. You prove that you listen, and energy flows freely between you. Your clients confide in you. Their trust and respect for you grows, and your relationships strengthen and flourish. Critical listening is a fundamental element of your communications.

You connect with your clients no matter the venue size. You extend an arm toward your client as you cast your eyes upon them and hold the contact as you deliver and complete your point. You look and dress the part—successful, impressive, classy, and respectful. You're firmly grounded whether seated or standing, and you gesture with ease and in synchrony with your message. You see and are seen in a new light.

Your voice projects not merely words, but emotions. You vary your pace and your tone for full effect. You let yourself pause—to think, to reflect, and to recharge; you let yourself pause—to pique your clients' curiosity, to draw them closer, to let them absorb. And you respect your clients and yourself by expunging non-words and hedge words from your speech. You have found your voice.

You understand that while style is a critical, so is command of substance. You've perfected clear and concise explanations of recurring subjects in plain, simple English, and enveloped them with the facts and feelings relating to each client's case to make them relevant. You support your position with statistics and analytics, patiently teaching instead of bewildering, and you paint visual imagery with your stories and analogies that touch your clients' hearts and minds.

You are proud to explain what you bring to each client relationship, you trust your disciplined process to find wealth management solutions in each of the four cornerstones, and you are committed to helping your clients build, manage, protect, and transition their wealth.

Your mastery of the critical elements of communication bestows upon you great power to exert on behalf of your clients. You use that power wisely and always in your clients' best interests—with care, skill, and caution—to help them succeed financially.

Indeed, you *have* learned to dance.

INDEX